Advance Praise for Activism, Inc.

❝ This book describes how grassroots politics has withered and what must be done to revive it. A timely message for America in the 21st century."

—Former U.S. Senator Bill Bradley

❝ Dana Fisher's *Activism, Inc.* is an extraordinarily important and incisive book, both readable and extremely well informed. An insider's look at today's civic activism and Democratic Party campaigns, it could well catalyze a national debate on the future and nature of progressive politics."

—Harry C. Boyte, Co-Director,
Center for Democracy and Citizenship, Humphrey Institute of Public Affairs

❝ What a delicious political irony! Progressivism, champion of the 'little person,' has organized its grassroots outreach like a 19th-century meat-packing plant, burning out young workers with low pay, long hours, and regimented, alienating working conditions. In this imminently readable, insightful volume, Dana Fisher brings us face to face with this counterintuitive state of affairs. Conservatives may draw some comfort from it. But as Americans, we should all be alarmed at the pitiless strip-mining of our young peoples' idealism."

—William A. Schambra, Director,
Bradley Center for Philanthropy and Civic Renewal, Hudson Institute

❝ An original grass roots critique as to why progressive citizen groups and the Democratic Party are failing to prevail and weakening themselves. Dana Fisher argues that you cannot outsource democratic movements. Listen up, national progressive groups, Fisher's insights are lighting up the path to greater effectiveness. Democrats also would be well advised to put this book at the top of their reading list. That is, if they want to understand better how to win elections."

—Ralph Nader

" For idealistic young progressives today there is basically only one paid entry-level job left in politics: canvassing. Dana Fisher is the first to study this crucial formative experience. Essentially she finds that the canvass is an alienating and undemocratic experience. As a result, we are squandering the energy and ideas of a whole generation. What's more, a progressive movement that relies on regimented canvassing is doomed to defeat because it lacks an authentic connection with citizens. Unless we take seriously the rigorous evidence and acute arguments of *Activism, Inc.*, the future looks grim."

—Peter Levine, Director,
The Center for Information & Research on Civic Learning & Engagement,
University of Maryland

" This is a provocative and sobering account of progressive politics in contemporary America enlivened by the stories of the no-longer so idealistic young canvassers. A must read for anyone who believes that youth activism inevitably deepens one's commitment to civic participation and who cares about the health and well-being of grassroots politics in the United States."

—Doug McAdam, Stanford University, author of *Freedom Summer*

Activism, Inc.

Activism, Inc.

How the Outsourcing of Grassroots Campaigns
Is Strangling Progressive Politics in America

Dana R. Fisher

Stanford University Press
Stanford, California 2006

Stanford University Press
Stanford, California

Printed in the United States of America on acid-free, archival-quality paper

Library of Congress Cataloging-in-Publication Data

Library of Congress Cataloging-in-Publication Data

Fisher, Dana, 1971-
  Activism, inc. : how the outsourcing of grassroots campaigns is strangling
progressive politics in America / Dana R. Fisher.
    p. cm.
  Includes bibliographical references and index.
  ISBN-13: 978-0-8047-5217-6 (cloth : alk. paper)
  1. Political participation--United States. 2. Political activists--United States.
3. Social movements--United States. I. Title.
JK1764.F527 2006
322.40973--dc22

                                                       2006009398

Designed by Bruce Lundquist

Typeset at Stanford University Press in 9.5/15 Minion

Contents

Acknowledgments

F irst and foremost, I would like to thank those institutes that supported research on this never-before-studied aspect of progressive politics: the Center for Information and Research on Civic Learning and Engagement (CIRCLE), which took a chance on a young academic and funded the first component of this study; the Institute for Social and Economic Research and Policy (ISERP) at Columbia University, which supported my data collection in Washington, D.C.; and the Council for Research in the Social Sciences at Columbia University, which supported my work during the summer of 2005 while I wrote up the findings of this project.

In addition, many people provided assistance and intellectual support. Lew Friedland has been an on-going sounding board for my ideas. In countless phone conversations, he has helped me apply the complex theoretical ideas that I first learned about in his graduate seminars at the University of Wisconsin–Madison to the challenges facing real-world politics today. I would also like to thank: Harry Boyte, who encouraged me to apply for funding to study canvassers in the first place and recognized the importance of this project from the beginning; Sid Tarrow and Debra Minkoff for their helpful comments on Chapter 1; and Paul-Brian McInerney, who provided an additional set of eyes and ears throughout the project and helped me collect and analyze loads of data to understand the role that canvassers play in civil society today. Lesley Wood, Lorien Jasny, and Paul Mazzilli provided valuable research assistance, as did the students in my courses on civil society, who heard more about canvassing than they ever cared to know.

Beyond these people, this book project benefited from the assistance of my agent, Giles Anderson, who helped me formulate my ideas early on. My editor at Stanford University Press, Kate Wahl, provided thoughtful comments on multiple drafts of chapters. I also want to thank my friend Kelly Notaras, who put me in touch with Giles in the first place.

Last, but not least, I would like to express my appreciation to my family and friends, who put up with my unavailability during my first three summers at Columbia. In particular, I want to thank my sister Carley, who canvassed with me for a short time during the summer of 1990 and reflected on her experiences with me as I developed this project and wrote the manuscript that became this book.

Finally, I must express my gratitude to my Aaron, who spent the summer of 2003 living alone while I collected data around the country and endured countless evenings talking about canvassers and progressive politics in America. I could not ask for a better partner, editor, and friend.

Raven Rock, N.J.
September 2005

Preface

After my first year at Princeton University, I was accepted into the university's Princeton-in-France summer program that began in June 1990. In order to make some spending money for the trip, I looked for a job near my parents' house outside Philadelphia. Attracted by an ad in the newspaper about jobs for the environment, I applied and interviewed at a grassroots campaign office near the train station; they hired me on the spot.

I found the office atmosphere contagious—young people home from colleges around the country came to this office to help the campaign to tighten controls on sulfur dioxide emissions in the Clean Air Act. I made friends quickly with these like-minded individuals, spending every evening out with them celebrating our progress toward saving the world. The experience was so life-altering that I called the coordinator of Princeton-in-France and lied, telling her I had contracted mono and could not participate in the program. I spent the rest of the summer field-managing a group of canvassers and going door-to-door throughout eastern Pennsylvania.

Without access to a bathroom and armed only with a clipboard and a petition, I spent my days knocking on people's doors asking them if they would contribute money to the campaign. I even organized a bicycle canvass in a previously uncanvassed part of rural Pennsylvania. The Clean Air Act was reauthorized the following November, and I knew that I had helped make it happen. Returning to school in the fall, I promptly dropped French and focused my coursework on environmental studies.

After graduation in 1993, I moved to Washington, D.C., to work in progressive politics during the first term of the Clinton administration.

I took what was described to me as a "lobbyist trainee" position with a national progressive group. When I arrived in D.C., however, I learned that, before I would be allowed to do any real political work, I would have to earn my stripes as a director of a door-to-door fundraising effort. Disappointed that I could not apply my environmental studies background to work on the legislative process, I found a position at a small environmental group where I *would* learn how to lobby. Other people, however, were not so lucky.

Another member of my class at Princeton, Stewart (a pseudonym), had also taken a job with the same national progressive group because he wanted to get involved in politics. Out of a sense of duty, he lasted much longer than I did as a director in the Washington canvass office. Within six months, however, Stewart "got frustrated with the fact that success was measured by dollars brought in and not by people convinced,"[1] and burned out on the sixty-plus-hour weeks coordinating a fleet of so-called foot soldiers for the campaign. He decided that politics wasn't for him and went back to school for a law degree. Although canvassing had taken some of the bounce out of his step, he told me it had not squelched all of his idealism. After practicing law for six years, Stewart realized that he wanted to become a teacher. When I caught up with him in the fall of 2005, he was just beginning his second year teaching fourth-graders in Massachusetts. In an e-mail message to me, he rejoiced: "And best of all, I'm finally 'saving the world' and genuinely contributing to making the world a better place."

Since 1993, as I moved out of my twenties and figured out what I wanted to do with my life, I was haunted by my experience trying to make a difference by working in progressive politics. As a result, during my first year at Columbia University, I wrote a proposal to study how the experience of canvassing affects young people. With funding from the Center for Information and Research on Civic Learning and Engagement (CIRCLE), I spent 2003 and 2004 studying a cohort of canvassers employed by one of the largest canvassing organizations in the country: the People's Project.[2] As canvassers, these young people went door to door or stood on sidewalks recruiting and renewing memberships for progressive national organizations, just as I had done. In the intervening ten years, however, this form of grassroots politics had become consolidated: these young people recruited members for top national environmental, consumer, human rights, and child-assistance groups. Although they appear to be working for different organizations, they are, in fact, working for one organization that runs canvasses for many national and state groups. In the summer of 2003, for example, the People's Project ran campaigns around the country for more than fifteen groups. From an approved list of forty-one canvass offices the Project ran that summer, I randomly selected one canvass office in each of the six regions of the United States to study.

During the summer of 2003, along with two graduate research assistants, I spent a week in each of these cities: Boulder, Colorado; Portland, Oregon; San Diego, California; Ann Arbor, Michigan; Baltimore, Maryland; and Atlanta, Georgia. At each site I interviewed and surveyed every canvasser in the office who was willing to participate and had completed the organization's requisite three-day training period. In all, I formally interviewed and surveyed 115 canvassers.[3] During the second half of 2004, I conducted follow-up telephone interviews with approximately two-thirds of this sample of 2003 summer canvassers.[4] The purpose of these phone conversations was for them to reflect on their experiences with the canvass and to talk about their political and civic involvement since our initial meeting in 2003. Thanks to additional funding provided by Columbia University's Institute for Social and Economic Research and Policy (ISERP), I was also able to travel to Washington, D.C. to interview representatives of national progressive groups that had hired the People's Project to run their grassroots campaigns in 2003, as well as political consultants who had worked on the 2004 presidential campaign.

My conversations with these idealistic young people around the country made me realize how much their experiences play into the challenges facing progressive politics in America today. It also became clear to me that the outsourcing of grassroots activism had extended beyond issue-based politics on the left and now includes aspects of electoral politics as well.

As the 2004 presidential election was heating up, an old friend invited me up to Boston to attend an event in honor of grassroots firms during the

Democratic National Convention. At the event, I learned that the People's Project had spun off a for-profit firm that was running fundraising canvasses for the Democratic Party. While there, I also ran into two people I had interviewed at canvass offices in 2003. Because the outsourcing of activism had expanded to a number of aspects of the 2004 presidential election, I took the opportunity to interview political consultants who were involved in the 2004 presidential election on the left about the grassroots tactics of the campaign. To compare these tactics with those of the Right, which had received significant attention in the media, I also spoke with a number of people who had worked on the campaign to reelect President George W. Bush.

This book is the product of every meeting and conversation I had with canvassers, representatives of national progressive groups, and political operatives on the left and the right. It tells the story of grassroots politics in America, focusing on the significant differences between the ways the Right and the Left reach out to their grassroots base and incorporate young people, for better and for worse.

Activism, Inc.

Chapter 1

The Man, the Message, and the Members
The 3Ms of Politics in America Today

I bumped into my former student Laura on Columbia's campus the winter after she graduated. She had recently returned from working in Minnesota for the Kerry campaign. Besides the fact that her long dark hair was now pixie short, she looked the same. The year before, as a history major, Laura had been one of the most outspoken and memorable students in my undergraduate sociology class. While writing her senior thesis, she had also participated in my graduate seminar on civil society, sometimes even challenging the graduate students to apply their ideas to the real world.

After graduation, Laura looked for a job in progressive politics. Although she found paid work at a new group that was focused on veterans' rights and participated in political events around New York City, she felt as if her efforts didn't really matter: everyone said New York would go for Kerry anyway. She heard from people who were working on the Kerry campaign that the best thing she could do, as a "blue state" resident, was donate money to help the campaign in the so-called swing states. Because she didn't have any money to give, Laura decided to move out to Minnesota for the final months of the campaign. Through an old friend who was working on the Kerry campaign, Laura got an unpaid job that turned into paid work by mid-September. "I went to Minnesota," she explained, "pretty convinced that Kerry was not going to win . . . That was probably a large reason for why I went . . . If I didn't go to Minnesota or do something drastic where I knew I was really doing *something*, I would feel as if it were my fault for the rest of my life."

When she arrived in St. Paul, Laura joined a number of other New Yorkers who had come out to help the campaign in any way they could. She worked seven days a week and, during the last few weeks, recalled sleeping about two hours a night and grabbing naps under her desk. If Kerry won, she and others on the campaign staff in Minnesota had been promised paid jobs in the White House.

In the fallout of the election on November 3, Laura was in shock. She didn't know what to tell the volunteers she had managed. After weeks of persuading them "to get up at five o'clock in the morning to hold signs on the highway, or to knock on doors," she found herself at a loss for words. Many of the volunteers had given up what she considered "real jobs" to work for the campaign. Comparing herself to these "real" people, she told me: "It's easy for someone who is so young and is relatively rootless to move to another state for a few months and do whatever they could and come back, because I had nothing to lose. I didn't have a job, I didn't have a family, and these people had that."

Unable to make sense of the election's outcome, Laura took the "fastest flight out of there . . . and moved back home." The new pixie haircut she sported when I ran into her shortly thereafter was the result of her experience on the campaign. She told me: "I was really wondering if anything I had done in Minnesota was for any good." Upon returning to New York, she had cut off all her hair and donated it to the nonprofit organization Locks of Love, which provides hairpieces for disadvantaged children: "I felt like by donating my hair, at least I knew something I had done was going for something good . . . even if it was . . . totally unrelated and it was such a small drop in a huge bucket."[1]

Laura resumed her job search but found that many of the paid jobs for which she was eligible involved raising money by going door to door. She summarized her options: "In order to enter any type of organization . . . you had to start as a canvasser . . . You got a very [low] base salary . . . more than that, you just got 50 percent of what you raised . . . So, I didn't take that job, I was just hoping for something better."

After spending more than $100,000 on an Ivy League education, Laura was unable to find a job in progressive politics that would take advantage of her intelligence and unfettered idealism. Her underwhelming list of paid political job options seemed unjust to me, considering her talents and education, but Laura just felt disappointed that she couldn't start making a difference right away and get a paycheck. Despite the many high-ranking political contacts she had made on the campaign trail, finding paid work in progressive politics after the election was just as difficult as it had been before she moved out to Minnesota.

After a few more months searching, she finally found some other options. She was offered a paid job with a national nonprofit in New York and, at the same time, she was invited to work for a leading progressive activist in Washington, D.C. The choice was between meaningful political work as an unpaid intern and salaried employment advertised as involving project work, research, and writing. Because the job in D.C. was unpaid, she found herself unable to turn down the $30,000-a-year job in New York.

Laura's experience in the five months after taking the job, however, did not meet her expectations. When I met with her to catch up in the summer of 2005, she bragged that she had become an expert copier: "Most of what I've been doing is copying, faxing, filing, maintaining databases, answering phones, and sending out packages." I was dismayed to hear that the young woman who had wowed me with her critiques of environmental projects in New York City was now a copy monkey with a flashier job title. Because of her on-going frustration at the dearth of job options in progressive politics, Laura planned to take the LSAT in the fall and apply to law schools.

Unfortunately, the year-long odyssey of this motivated young Ivy League graduate attempting to break into left-leaning politics in America is not unique. While the Right provides numerous opportunities for interested young people to become embedded in its extensive political infrastructure,[2] those who want to work on the other side, like Laura, find a very limited number of entry points. This book is about young people like Laura and the ways the political organization of the Left has narrowed the channels of entry into progressive politics in America. Through personal contacts made at Columbia and an elite public high school in New York City, Laura's experience has been better than that of most people her age: she has had choices. But for too many members of this generation of potential progressive leaders, the outsourcing of grassroots activism to a handful of national groups has left them excluded, exploited, and disinterested in politics as a whole.

The 3Ms: Making Sense of the Failure of the Left in the 2004 Election

Political consultants, talking heads, and members of the media have pointed to several differences between the Left and the Right to explain the outcome of the 2004 election. Three of these explanations have received the majority of the attention. They can be summarized by what I call "*the three Ms*:" (1) the *Man*, (2) the *Message*, and (3) the *Members*. Attention to these three aspects of the campaign have come from all sides.

People who work inside the Beltway (the highway that surrounds Washington D.C., the nation's capital), including the politicos who run campaigns, think tanks, and advocacy groups, explain the Left's failure in the 2004 presidential election mainly by focusing on the differences between the *men* who were the candidates for the office. Even the political insiders who ran the Democratic campaign found John Kerry to be an uninspiring candidate. Tom Lindenfeld, a Democratic political consultant who was one of the architects of America Coming Together for the 2004 presidential election,[3] gave me his take on the election's outcome when I met with him in May 2005:

> We had a bad messenger, just as Mondale or Dukakis or any number of other bad Democratic candidates have also been . . . It's damn hard to pull a candidate who is not able to connect through [to a victory]. I think we had enormous inroads . . . and overcame an enormous amount . . . [For example, Kerry] got a greater turnout of African American voters than did Gore, than did Clinton, and other people who have had, indeed, a greater connection. And that, in my opinion, speaks to the organizational capacity that overcame the candidate's inabilities.

These opinions extended well beyond the democratic political consultants who ran components of Kerry's campaign and the privately funded 527 political groups that tried to influence the outcome of the election. John Passacantando, the executive director of Greenpeace USA, for example, also blamed the candidate: "John Kerry had plenty of money . . . [but] it wasn't a fight about money, not at all. George Bush believed more deeply and connected better." These views have been repeated by a handful of media outlets, such as the *Progressive* and *Salon*.[4] An observation by the left-wing blog the *Decembrist* provided one popular perspective: "Kerry just doesn't make a great first impression."[5]

In contrast to Kerry, Bill Clinton was said to be so charismatic and so inspiring that the Democratic Party could just sit back and relax during the election of 1992. In the words of Josh Wachs, who served as the executive director of the Democratic National Committee from 2002 to 2005: "Bill Clinton was such an effective spokesperson for the party, all you needed to do was put him out there and put a microphone in front of him." In fact, many critiques of the failed Gore campaign in 2000 blamed Gore's unwillingness to let Clinton help him campaign.[6] And when Clinton ended up in the hospital for emergency heart surgery in September 2004, Democrats across the country worried that the former president's inability to stump for Kerry would affect the outcome of the election.

Sitting back and relying on such a charismatic candidate can be problematic; only people with charisma can use it to their advantage, and it is unclear whether elected officials who win by means of charisma have strong political coattails. As former New Jersey senator Bill Bradley wrote in the *New York Times*, "A party based on charisma has no long-term impact." Reflecting on the Clinton presidency, Bradley noted: "The president did well. The party did not. Charisma didn't translate into structure."[7]

In addition, charismatic candidates such as Clinton come along very rarely. Former Vermont governor and presidential candidate Howard Dean, for example, was originally seen as such a candidate. But he was not as disciplined as Clinton about his public persona and, upon learning that he had come in third in the Iowa primary, he let out a primal scream that was picked up by websites and media outlets; those who opposed him used it as "proof" that he was not fit to be president. Dean subsequently lost the confidence of many Democratic voters as well as the party machine. Ironically, although he was not considered an appropriate presidential candidate, Dean took over as the chairman of the Democratic National

Committee in February of 2005. In addition, the now infamous "I Have a Scream" speech gained cult-like status on the Web, spawning musical remixes and comedic videos.[8]

In the media, however, the difference between the two candidates' *messages* has been the major explanation for the Left's failure in the 2004 election. Media outlets and talking heads have focused ad nauseam on "moral values" and how the Bush campaign's morally inspired message more effectively mobilized voters.[9] As a result of the uproar over the moral values issue, books such as Thomas Frank's *What's the Matter with Kansas?* have become must-reads for any left-leaning American who is trying to make sense of President Bush's reelection. In his afterword, which was added after the election, Frank, the founding editor of the independent magazine *The Baffler*, concludes that the Republicans won as a result of the success of the narrative of *backlash conservatism*. In Frank's opinion, the message was successfully transmitted to the American public that "George W. Bush was authentic; John Forbes Kerry, like all liberals, was an affected toff, a Boston Brahmin who knew nothing of the struggles of average folks."[10] In other words, the Bush campaign did a better job presenting a credible story and creating a persona for their candidate.

The importance of the message to a campaign is also emphasized in the words of political consultant Tom Lindenfeld: "It's about the quality of the communication and the ability for it to hit to the bone and be remembered."[11] Attention to the message and the way it is framed in politics has contributed to the metamorphosis of UC Berkeley professor of linguistics George Lakoff into a sought-after political consultant. Since the publication of his book *Don't Think of an Elephant*, which is subtitled "the essential guide for progressives" and explains how progressives should use language to frame the political debate, Lakoff has been thrust into the stratosphere of the political lecture circuit.[12]

Although the message can be controlled and spun, messages that do not resonate with the *members* of a political base do not work. Therefore, although the message is important, it is the members that matter, for they are the voters. To be sure, what voters do and how they do it continues to be determined, not by the nation's taste-makers or political public relations firms, but by the citizens themselves and the communities in which they live. It is this aspect of politics that is commonly referred to as *the grassroots*. During the 2004 election, the media began to recognize the importance of the grassroots in this race, focusing on the so-called *ground war*. In a *New York Times* article published during the election, this aspect of the campaign was said to be "back after a long hiatus, subtly changing politics as we know it."[13]

The notion of the grassroots was born of the idea that politics must be grounded in the convictions of everyday citizens who are rooted in their localities. In other words, in contrast to the *man* (or woman) who runs for office and the *message* that his or her political campaign promotes, the *members* are not controllable by the campaign. As much as political consultants would like to think the framing of the message or an exceptionally charismatic candidate is all that matters, it is the opinions of the citizen base that decides elections.[14] In the 2004 election, the types of connections that each campaign had with local people on the grassroots level around the country played a significant role in the election's outcome, prompting many to think about what *meaningful participation* in politics is and how one mobilizes a membership base.[15]

Understanding Meaningful Membership

In recent years, scholars have lamented the lack of Americans' civic and political engagement. Contrary to earlier observations about the vibrant civic life of Americans,[16] citizens have become disconnected from one another and detached from the world around them. These findings are well known, in part because of Robert Putnam's widely cited work *Bowling Alone*, in which he writes that, in contrast to earlier eras when Americans bowled in teams made up of neighbors and friends, today they bowl (and do many other things) alone: "Americans today feel vaguely and uncomfortably disconnected."[17] Similarly, in the updated edition of their well-known work *Habits of the Heart*, Robert Bellah and his coauthors find that public life in America is fading amid increasing pressure to disengage from American society.[18]

There have been some countertrends. Theda Skocpol, who is a colleague of Putnam's at Harvard, has studied the ways Americans do engage.

She finds that "Americans *are* finding new ways to relate to one another and accomplish shared tasks." Nevertheless, she concludes that there has been a shift from *membership* to *management* in American civic life.[19] In this work, she focuses on the transition of American civil society away from nationally federated and locally grounded civic groups to what has come to be known as "mail-in membership" in tertiary associations. These associations include national groups, such as the Association for the Advancement of Retired Persons (AARP), professional organizations such as the American Bar Association, and interest groups such as the National Wildlife Federation. There are numerous such organizations and associations to which Americans contribute money and receive, in return, membership cards and magazines. Many of these organizations use their lengthy membership lists to influence policymakers, reminding them that their constituents might not reelect them if they do not support a certain bill or approve funding for a particular issue.

Beyond receiving a membership card, which may or may not entitle members to discounts on hotels, car rentals, and the like, more and more national membership-based groups ask their members to share their e-mail addresses.[20] In many instances, members who provide their e-mail addresses are asked to participate in "e-actions," such as sending e-mails to congressional representatives, senators, or the president. This type of armchair activism received significant attention with the emergence of the Internet-focused organization MoveOn.org, which rose to prominence during the public debate over the potential impeachment of President Clinton in 1998.[21]

Such armchair activists also fueled the frenzy over Howard Dean's bid for the Democratic presidential nomination in 2004. Through its website, the Dean campaign raised a large amount of money from small donations by average Americans. More recently, this type of civic involvement has supported relief efforts for victims of the December 2004 tsunami in Asia, and for hurricane Katrina in August 2005.[22] Citizens have only to click a link on the website of their bank or favorite radio station to contribute money to aid the victims of these natural disasters. Although these efforts have been very successful in raising money, it is unclear whether this type of support and membership in national groups that are disconnected from local chapters and local meetings is anything more than symbolic.[23] As Jeffrey Berry points out in his work on such groups, "These organizations require no active involvement on the part of their members."[24] Even though such interest groups originally formed to "link policy outcomes to political concerns" of the public,[25] the circuit has become severed.

It is this disconnection between national groups and their members that Margaret Weir and Marshall Ganz focus on in their assessment of progressive politics after the 1996 presidential election. Building on Skocpol's finding that there are few connections between national interest groups and the political base that these groups purport to represent, the authors find that, even though professional advocacy-oriented groups are growing in number, they "have lost much of their popular base, focusing instead on Washington-based, staff-led activities." This type of membership does not necessarily translate into *meaningful* participation such as voting or other political activity. As Weir and Ganz conclude: "Politics and policymaking have become unanchored, susceptible to pressures from more mobilized minorities."[26]

Morris Fiorina discusses such mobilized minorities in his work on "the dark side of civic engagement." He stresses that participation in the American political system today requires significant time and energy. As a result, he says, people active in political groups "come disproportionately from the ranks of those with intensely held extreme views."[27] In other words, members of national groups tend to hold more mainstream views than the few active participants and staff people who run national political campaigns.

In contrast to these trends in progressive politics, the Republican Party, as well as the Right more broadly, has developed tools to create lasting connections with its political base.[28] Adopting more and more of the platform originally developed by the Christian Coalition, Republicans are able to tap into the extensive network of local groups that the Coalition developed since its creation by Pat Robertson in the late 1980s.[29] These trends were observed by the media as far back as 1993, when Greg Goldin published an article about "How the Christian Right Is Building from Below to Take Over from Above."[30]

In the 2004 presidential election, the Bush-Cheney campaign instituted a strategy designed to exploit such local connections. As a result of its "72-hour plan," which gained notoriety when *New York Times* journalist Matt Bai likened it to the Amway model of multilevel marketing, the Right is not facing a crisis of membership.[31] Instead, the Republican Party has used the 72-hour plan to take advantage of these ever-expanding networks of conservative Americans. As a result, there has been what the *Christian Statesman* called a Christianization of the Republican Party. By fall 2002, the *Christian Statesman*, which focuses on what it calls "explicitly Christian politics," reported: "Christian conservatives have become a staple of politics nearly everywhere. Christian conservatives now hold a majority of seats in 36% of all Republican Party state committees (or 18 of 50 states), plus large minorities in 81% of the rest, double their strength from a decade before."[32]

Because of their growing influence, ideological conservatives have mobilized effectively around national political debates related to abortion, same-sex marriage, stem cell research, and judicial nominees. Also, based on efforts by conservative Christians to "train a new generation of Christian politicians,"[33] their influence in politics is likely to increase in the coming years. In contrast to the relatively fragmented coalition of mobilized minorities on the left, the Right is being driven to a large extent by densely connected and locally rooted conservative Christians who constitute an estimated 25 percent of the American population.[34]

While the Right expands through these dense local networks, the Left is trying to overcome the weakening connections between local members and the national progressive groups that represent them. One of the main ways that the Left is responding to this challenge is by consolidating its grassroots campaigns. But the way the Left runs these campaigns through professional organizations that hire young people to canvass for them is having a significant effect on the thousands of young people who work as paid canvassers. The experiences they have in those jobs are shaping the future of progressive politics in the United States and determining the ways these Americans will participate in politics in the future.

A Brief History of Canvassing in America

To understand the impact of the Left's grassroots campaigns on their young employees and on progressive politics in the United States more broadly, we must begin at the beginning: what is a canvass and what does it do? Harry Boyte, a senior adviser to the National Commission on Civic Renewal, describes the purpose of the canvass: it is "a method for large scale [citizen] mobilizations to counter corporate pressure to roll back environmental, consumer, affirmative action, and other government regulations."[35] The canvass epitomizes the connection between local organizing and national politics: many canvasses are nationally coordinated and aim to achieve broad political goals through the mobilization of local citizens.

Canvassing was originally developed as a tactic for registering and contacting voters. It involves walking from house to house and speaking directly with citizens at their front doors. In *Get Out the Vote!*, a guide to increasing voter turnout, Donald Green and Alan Gerber explain that "door-to-door canvassing was once the bread and butter of party mobilization, particularly in urban areas."[36] This method of contacting voters became a key tool of the civil rights movement. In 1964, college students from across the United States traveled to Mississippi to go door to door, registering African Americans to vote during what became known as Freedom Summer.[37] Although political campaigns have relied more on direct mail and phone solicitation in recent years, organizations supportive of both of the major candidates in the 2004 presidential campaign coordinated thousands of volunteers who flooded swing states to canvass during the days leading up to November 2, 2004.[38]

Canvassing to recruit members for progressive organizations is an offshoot of electoral canvassing. After volunteering for the campaign to elect a reformist alderman in Chicago's 44th ward in 1970, an encyclopedia salesman named Marc Anderson decided to combine his door-to-door sales knowledge with his political experience. Speaking with me in the summer of 2005, he explained his motivation: "If you can sell books to people door to door, you can certainly use the same discipline to talk politics and issues." The goal was to develop a funding mechanism for environmental groups. Anderson observed: "What they seemed to be short on was not strategy and not great power, but money. So I used the door-to-door canvassing to raise money." Through his newly founded group, Citizens for a Better Environment, Anderson discovered that, in addition to raising money, speaking to citizens at their doors was an ideal way to spread the word about the political agenda of the environmental movement.

With his success at Citizens for a Better Environment and the Illinois Public Action Council, which he founded to work on a broader diversity of campaigns, word of this new form of fundraising spread. Anderson recalled being asked to help other progressive groups set up their own canvassing programs. By the mid-1970s, he was getting so many requests that he left the Illinois Public Action Council and founded the Hudson Bay Company of Illinois. The mission of this new group was to raise money and help other nonprofit groups create outreach programs of their own. He explained to me: "We started mostly with environmental groups, but we also worked with NARAL [the National Abortion and Reproductive Rights Action League], women's groups, and consumer groups." Over the years, the Hudson Bay Company has helped progressive groups around the United States develop and maintain a grassroots base for their national campaigns.[39]

A Harvard law student who had been working with Ralph Nader on water issues, David Zwick, became intrigued by Anderson's success. In May 2005, Zwick told me that he was originally inspired by the story of the populist agrarian movement of the early 1900s.[40] He founded Clean Water Action with support from fishing and tackle companies,[41] but the money ran out before the job was done. Zwick told me he "ended up thinking: Boy, this isn't going to get solved in Washington alone. There has to be a base, there has to be an organized base."

After the money ran out, this self-described Nader's Raider started doing research on canvassing as a potential means of developing such an organized base. Because the Hudson Bay Company was contractually prevented from working with any other groups in the Washington, D.C., area, Zwick was unable to hire it to start a canvass for his group. Instead, he went to Chicago to learn how the Hudson Bay Company worked. Besides observing Anderson's outfit, Zwick prepared by "reading books about selling vacuum cleaners door to door." Through his work, Clean Water Action ended up developing a successful canvass. Since then, Zwick has become known as a "pioneer of the [canvassing] method."[42]

Zwick and Anderson agree that all of the issue-based groups that have canvassed over the past thirty-plus years can be traced back to Anderson's work, either via his direct management of their canvass or through people he trained, who spun off to run canvasses for other groups. The former encyclopedia salesman reflected on the contribution he has made to progressive politics in America: "All those [groups that are] canvassing all came eventually from Citizens for a Better Environment and [the] Hudson Bay Company. There were not any other people who were doing it independent of us." He recalls the birth of many progressive groups that canvassed to support their work by "splitting off one from another [and] starting new groups." David Zwick also noted that Anderson's work was the starting point for the progressive groups that have canvassed: "Virtually all . . . [groups] that [canvass] today are either imitators or direct descendants."

Thanks to these imaginative idealists, canvassing has developed into a mainstream tactic used by progressive groups to maintain a membership base and sustain their funding. Since the early 1990s, canvassing techniques have further evolved to include what has come to be called the "street canvass." In urban centers where going door to door is dangerous or impractical, or there is a lot of foot traffic, canvassers stand on streetcorners, where they stop people and ask whether they have time to support the campaign. In contrast to canvassers who go door to door collecting predominantly cash and checks, street canvassers ask people to become long-term supporters by providing a credit card number that can be charged monthly.

Today the majority of canvassers are paid employees who go door to door in the afternoons and early evenings, or stand on streetcorners, recruiting and renewing memberships for organizations that include top national environmental, consumer, human rights, and child-assistance groups. Because of the long hours, tiring work, and low pay, canvassers tend to be young people. They spend about six hours a day actually canvassing, but they must get to the office at least an hour before going out to "the field" and come back to the office after canvassing to record their results from the day and check out.

Even though canvasses are run year-round, the majority of canvassing gets done over the summer, when satellite campaign offices spring up all over the United States and hire college students to work during their vacations. Enticed by the idea that they could "be part of the solution" and "take their conscience to work," these young people spend their summer vacations going door to door or standing on the street, recruiting and renewing memberships for progressive groups. In any given summer, thousands of young people work at such campaign offices for progressive groups. In a 2002 study of the civic and political health of the nation, in fact, Scott Keeter and his colleagues found that over 7 percent of the study's participants between the ages of 15 and 37—or more than 5.5 million Americans—had participated in a canvass at one time or another.[43]

During the 1990s, when funding for progressive causes was limited, many national progressive groups closed their field offices, and some of these groups stopped running their own grassroots outreach programs.[44] David Zwick provided his interpretation: "The economics of it and the demographics of it have . . . weeded out a lot." In the late 1990s, the grassroots campaigns for left-leaning organizations became consolidated, with many progressive groups hiring intermediary organizations to run their local campaigns by canvassing.

Progressive groups that outsource no longer have to run local offices or train canvassers to conduct grassroots outreach. Instead, they have only to sign up with an intermediary organization and trained canvassers will go door to door or stand on the street on their behalf, dressed in the progressive group's T-shirt. It is easier and less expensive for a group to pay an intermediary organization to run these grassroots campaigns than for the group to do it itself. As national groups increasingly outsource to a handful of intermediary organizations, the distance between the members and the progressive national groups that claim to represent them has become greater than ever before.

The consolidation of grassroots activism exacerbates another challenge to progressive politics: its continued reliance on political consultants and professional organizers to run campaigns. By hiring political professionals and national canvassing firms, campaigns fail to become embedded in the local institutions and grassroots networks of civil society. A small number of studies have catalogued what Carmen Sirianni and Lewis Friedland call "civic innovation in America." Finding that this type of innovation involves the "experimentation by ordinary citizens and civic associations, supported by professional practitioners within and outside government," the authors conclude that a "civic renewal movement has begun to emerge."[45] These vibrant networks of local civic activity, however, tend to be completely overlooked by most progressive political campaigns, including these grassroots campaigns that involve canvassing. Although a few political consultants on the left have recognized that this neglect has serious implications for the quality of the campaigns, the practices of the Democratic Party have not changed. As one influential political consultant who worked on the Kerry campaign explained to me, many of the largest interest groups that influence Democratic politics "are not accustomed to really mobilizing their base, they don't really have a base, and they don't have relationships with their members." Paradoxically, this type of political involvement continues be the backbone of progressive grassroots politics in America today.

Focusing on the People's Project

To understand the effects that the consolidation of grassroots activism is having on progressive politics and young people like my former student Laura, this book presents data from research conducted on one of the largest national groups that runs canvasses in the United States: the People's Project.[46]

The People's Project started running canvasses in the early 1980s. By the 1990s it was coordinating campaigns for an array of national and state-level progressive groups. Today, as one of the largest canvassing organizations in America, the People's Project runs between fifty-five and seventy-five campaign offices around the country.[47] One national staff member estimated that the 2001 summer canvass had over 275 canvass directors who oversaw the thousands of young people who participated in it. My visits to canvass offices around the country suggest that the 2003 canvass was of a similar size.

The sheer volume of this grassroots effort allows the People's Project to run campaigns for multiple progressive groups. During the summer of 2003, it ran canvasses that addressed poverty alleviation, legal rights for same-sex partners, and many different environmental goals. When the Democratic Party began to run an outsourced canvass, in fact, it hired a for-profit spinoff that had been started by one of the founders of the People's Project.[48]

The size of each office varies each summer and each day—from huge operations like the Portland, Oregon, office (which had more than seventy canvassers in 2003) to the Baltimore office (fewer than five canvassers). In addition, the grassroots reach of each campaign office varies. Some offices send canvassers more than an hour away to garner support for local and national political initiatives. While I was visiting the Portland campaign office in July 2003, it was running what it called a "camping canvass" more than a hundred miles away in Idaho. The canvassers camped in a park at night and canvassed during the day.

The People's Project attracts politically concerned young people, many of whom know how to become involved in politics but lack the time or incentive to act alone. It provides them with an opportunity to express their political beliefs and get paid for their work. In many ways, the Project channels canvassers' politics and practices according to larger organizational goals. Canvassers and higher-level staff consider themselves activists, but activism has a very specific meaning in the context of the organization: going door to door to generate support for the issue of the day in the form of members and money. Canvassers do not march in the streets or take part in rallies, at least not on the Project's time; to be a canvasser is to be a foot soldier for the campaign. Beyond raising money, canvassers are expected to write letters to politicians on selected issues and submit opinion pieces to local newspapers—in both cases, the People's Project provides form letters the canvasser may use or customize.

Also, canvassers are expected to participate in press conferences held by their offices. At the Project's campaign office in Atlanta, I observed a press conference that included a twenty-one-chainsaw "salute" in opposition to the Bush administration's forest policies. The press conference was coordinated with a larger one run by the national office in Washington, D.C., which had devised the strategy as well as the concept and text for the event. Each campaign office had only to rent the chainsaws, call the targeted media outlets, and read the text in front of the media. In order to save money, the Atlanta office decided to rent only seven chainsaws.

The event that I observed was embarrassingly underattended and unsuccessful. After about fifteen minutes of trying to start the chainsaws, the group was about to give up when some construction workers eating their lunches nearby laughingly offered their assistance and started one of the chainsaws. In the end, only two chainsaws were started and no members of the press showed up. As I walked away from the event, the only evidence that the "chainsaw salute" had even occurred was the puddle of spilled gasoline left on the sidewalk in front of the government office.

A major effect of this consolidation of grassroots activism is that it severely limits the entry points for young people like Laura, the former student of mine who want to get involved in progressive politics. As a national coordinator of the canvass pointed out to me, after working as a successful canvasser for the organization, canvassers are both funneled into leadership positions with the national canvassing office *and* guided into positions at any of a number of the national progressive groups for whom they run campaigns. Thus, for the thousands of young people who try out canvassing as a way of making a difference, the canvass is the gatekeeper to jobs in progressive politics. Although there are other ways for young people to get jobs with the national groups that have outsourced their grassroots campaigns, canvassing provides one of the only channels into these groups from the local level. For someone who cannot move to Washington to take an unpaid internship or who has no personal connections to an organization, canvassing also provides one of the few paid routes into national progressive politics in America. For this reason, the People's Project considers itself to be a training ground for progressive activists.

Although a handful of the young people who join the canvass find it an ideal job and stay with the organization, they are in the minority. Most don't make it past the first week, and many not past the first day. Because canvassing is very hard work and the organization expects long hours, many canvassers quickly burn out. Others become disenchanted with its system of grassroots activism, which relies on monetary quotas to gauge success. Through its bureaucratic/hierarchical structure, and its practice of burning through interested young people, this organization is having a significant negative effect on the left.

Given the failure of the Left to win elections in the national political arena and the disenchantment of many citizens these days, it is more important than ever to understand the ways that progressive Americans are *engaging* in politics. As civic disengagement increases, it is more and more important to understand what has happened to those young people who are the future of progressive politics in America.

In the wake of two difficult presidential elections and the scandals related to the war in Iraq, many Americans believe that no one listens when they express their dissatisfaction with the ways that politics are being practiced in the United States. As my students have pointed out in defense of their lack of political involvement: even when they participate along with millions of Americans in demonstrations against the war, nobody responds. Since they believe their opinions do not matter to the national government, they grow less and less interested in expressing them.

Therefore, with the People's Project creating what one canvasser called "a monopoly on political organizing" for the Left, we must understand the ways that young people experience politics through their work for these grassroots campaigns. This book is based on research about American politics at the grassroots and national levels and involves data collected through hundreds of conversations around the country from 2003 through 2005. In telling the story of this consolidation of activism on the left and comparing the grassroots campaigns of the Left with those of the Right, I discuss the implications of this process for America's youth and their current and future involvement in politics.

Today, too many progressive young Americans, who make up a whole generation of potential political leaders, are ending up turned off and burned out. As one organization consolidates grassroots campaigns for many of the major national progressive groups and serves as the gate-keeper for young people who want to work for them, it is imperative that we understand the effects this centralization of activism is having on progressive politics. Incorporating conversations with canvassers coupled with discussions with progressive leaders and those who ran both sides of the presidential campaign in 2004, I connect the process of outsourcing grassroots activism to the decline in progressive politics on the national stage. It is only through the combination of research at the grassroots and national levels that we can fully understand the relationship between national politics and the grassroots base, as well as the ways that the Left is failing to connect to its base and yield political success.

Chapter 2

Institutionalizing Activism

The People's Project

I arrived at the Portland canvass office exhausted. For some reason, the only way for me to fly from New York City to Portland, Oregon, get there before sunset, *and* earn frequent-flier miles was to go through Houston. So, I left my apartment at 4:45 on a Monday morning to arrive at the canvass office early enough to be introduced to the staff before the daily announcements began.

Entering the Portland office of the People's Project, I was impressed by its size: the campaign office occupied most of the first floor of a two-story industrial-looking building, with the group's regional lobbyists and other offices on the building's second floor. In comparison with the Baltimore and Atlanta offices, which I had already visited that summer, the Portland office was by far the biggest. A representative of the Project's national office, Jerry, had told me that the Portland canvass was one of the largest in the country, running both street and door-to-door campaigns simultaneously.[1] As a result, the office was sending out about seventy-five canvassers into Portland and its environs each day to garner support for the Project's campaigns.

Having picked up a double nonfat frozen latte at the café around the corner, I joined about fifty canvassers who were assembling in an open room at the back of the building. In all canvass offices, before going out to the field, canvassers assemble for their daily announcements. Door canvassers, who go door to door during the afternoon and early evening hours, hear announcements every day around 2:00 p.m. Street canvassers assemble for announcements earlier because they aim to recruit members during traditional business hours. As a result, the street canvassers in the office had already gone out when I arrived.[2]

Announcements serve multiple purposes for the campaign offices: they introduce observers and trainees to the office and its members, they review the campaign's targets, they summarize the office's progress toward those goals, they recognize the most successful canvassers from the previous day, and they split up the canvassers into crews for the day's work. They are also used as motivational sessions for canvassers before they go out to the field. In that regard, I was unprepared for the Portland office's particularly exuberant announcements, which involved chanting, singing, and dancing. Yes, dancing. Susie, who was managing the town of Hollywood, Oregon, began to call her crew for the day by jumping onto a table and dancing while people in the crowd sang the old theme song "Hooray for Hollywood."

After all of the canvassers and trainees had been assigned to crews for the day, one of the directors of the office asked me to introduce myself, explain my study, and invite everyone who had completed their training to sign up for a time to be interviewed. All of a sudden the cheering stopped. There was no more singing and dancing, just everyone in the room looking at me. Mustering as much perkiness as I could, I summarized the project, exaggerating my arm gestures in an effort to make being interviewed and surveyed seem less like guinea pig experiments and more like fun socializing.

After my pitch, announcements ended abruptly with a final cheer that sent the canvassers springing into action. Within minutes, the office had emptied out. The canvassers dispersed throughout the Portland metropolitan area to recruit and renew memberships for campaigns that included cleaning up a local river, protecting a stand of old-growth forest, and supporting disadvantaged children. In the hush after their departure, the graduate student who had traveled with me to help conduct the interviews, Paul-Brian, turned to me with wide eyes and said: "So, that's how it's supposed to work."

For the past few weeks, along with a graduate student, I had traveled from one canvass office to another interviewing and surveying canvassers and observing the way the offices were run. In every office we sat in on daily announcements. Although the accents of the people running the meetings differed around the country, as well as the level of ecstasy reached by the canvassers, it had become clear that the procedure had been standardized by the organization. I later realized that the entire experience—from the phone call to schedule an interview to the final exit discussion—is completely scripted. Canvass directors have only to follow the steps laid out in the handbooks provided by the People's Project to achieve the organization's goals. It has developed what one long-term canvasser called an "efficient model" for running a canvass, where they have taken "something this chaotic in canvassing and turn[ed] it into . . . a science" (Mike, 33, Atlanta canvass).

The specifics of this model were documented by a number of long-term canvassers. Harland, a 26-year-old who grew up in North Dakota and was considering becoming a Unitarian minister, had canvassed in the Portland office for over a year and, before moving to Oregon, had worked for over two years in a canvassing office in the Midwest. Harland's was the last interview I conducted on that long marathon Monday in Portland. During our discussion, he pointed out: "Everything's by the book, by the letter . . . This is how you deal with people, this is the time frame you work with, this is what has to happen every single day."

Roy had worked as a canvasser and a canvass director in the Portland office for over two years since graduating from a small liberal arts school on the East Coast. During his follow-up interview while he was working in the People's Project national office in 2004, he fondly recalled the structure of his days on the canvass: "Every day you answer the phone, you do the interviews at 10 . . . you do role plays from 1 to 2, you do announcements at 2, you eat lunch from 2 to 3, you canvass 4 to 9, and you cash out 9 to 10 . . . And it's the same every day and, while there [are] different challenges that arrive from your staff, the structure is the same . . . It's, you know, fairly regimented." The regimen Roy referred to is outlined to the directors during the organization's director training programs, which are held twice a year. Although Roy was describing the schedule of a canvass director, the day in the life of a canvasser is just as standardized.

For example, Mike, a 33-year-old with a graduate degree in journalism who had canvassed for the People's Project out of its Atlanta office for two years, also spoke about the level of standardization in the canvassing process during our follow-up discussion in 2004: "[They] have a very well-organized . . . step-by-step process that they use." Having worked as a canvass director for a local Greenpeace office in the 1990s, Mike appreciated the organization's process, but was concerned about how this standardization had affected the quality of the canvassing: "I think that it has misled [the People's Project] into thinking that they can teach anybody to be an effective environmental advocate, and that's simply not the case."

Creating Canvassers through the Training Process

No experience is needed to get hired as a canvasser for the People's Project, and the organization offers work to just about everyone who turns up for an interview. Once this motley crew of interested people comes through the door, however, they must be trained. The training process involves being an observer for a day; then, if the applicant is still interested in the job, there is a three-day training period. Canvassers who exceeded the quota set by the office during their first or second day canvassing reported having to train for less time. Training involves learning skills that are designed to make the canvassers comfortable recruiting and renewing members on the streets and at people's front doors. Its main goal is to prepare these young people sufficiently to become full-time staff members who consistently earn quota for their office's campaigns.

In contrast to how other organizations, such as Greenpeace, have run canvasses in the past, with a "constant issue focus . . . [where canvassers are] expected to know everything [they] could know about any issue" (Mike, 33, Atlanta canvass), the majority of the training to be a canvasser for the People's Project involves learning what to say. Canvassers recalled being trained from the start to memorize "the Script," and they were expected to recite the Script on the streetcorner or at the door.

Lisa, a director in the Portland office who had been employed by the Project for about three years, described it: "We have a standard [Script], so it's like everything is just written out for you, and we actually require that people say *exactly* what's there and memorize it, and it's really not that hard to memorize 'cuz it's not that long. It's less than two minutes . . . [and] it basically has the main points that we want to get across so . . . [canvassers are] sending out the same message." Canvassers from the offices I visited in the summer of 2003 praised the efficiency of the Script, declaring their confidence in it. They understood that it should be recited verbatim because it had been, as Bruce in the Ann Arbor canvass explained, "focus-grouped to death." Ironically, even though these canvassers were working as paid activists for a nonprofit organization that focused on progressive causes, a number of them referred to the Script as the Project's "sales pitch."

Although they were asked to recite the Script verbatim when they were canvassing, some canvassers did recollect deviating from it to make it more conversational and natural-sounding. Paul, a 20-year-old college student who had been working in the Portland office for three weeks, for example, explained why some canvassers went off Script:

> After a while, [the Script], which is what we say at the beginning to just kind of hook people and get as much information as possible out there for them, it becomes very automatic and I think you lose . . . or you're not conveying as much of your sincerity as you should. When you first get at it, you might be stumbling through the thing, but people really understand, you know, the sincerity of what you're doing comes out. If you're just kind of running through something, you sound like . . . a used car commercial 'cuz you're going really, really fast . . . I'm still as sincere, probably more sincere . . . now, because I know more about the organization and what it's doing. But, at the same time, it's like I'm not conveying that as well. It's a little bit too professional. People want something that they can understand.

In addition, a number of these young people expressed concern about the emphasis by the People's Project on the efficiency with which canvassers identified "sympathetic doors." In other words, the purpose of the Script was to present information quickly and efficiently so that they could effectively identify potential members and sign them up.

In addition to learning the Script, canvassers were taught how to manage various situations when presenting it. Some recalled being trained how to deal with interruptions during their pitch, how to respond to people who said they had no money, and how to increase the annual contribution of existing members. Both street and door canvassers stressed the importance of their body language and their greeting. Stephanie had been canvassing for the Atlanta office for over two years, sometimes training two canvassers in a day. When training new canvassers, she emphasized that "it's important to have a great greeting. It's important to smile, and it's important to be serious and earnest when there is something serious that you're talking about."

In fact, those who were working as street canvassers recalled spending a significant amount of their training time developing their greetings. Rebecca, who had been working for the People's Project for a year and was a director in the San Diego office in 2003, explained the focus of the training for street canvassers: Beyond learning the Script, she said, training for street canvassers focused on "greeting people [with] smiles and . . . [how to] ask them to stop, . . . how to be persuasive with people, how to use your judgment over your personal stance, and how to make it a positive experience for everyone involved."

Emily, a 20-year-old woman who had worked as a street canvasser for six days in the Portland office, provided her personal perspective on the importance of the greeting: "The biggest selling [point] is just having a really happy greeting and just saying 'hey, what's up, how are you doing, do you have a second to talk to me about this?'" But she also echoed Paul's concern about the verbatim recitation of the Script: "I think the hardest part is [that] you say it so many times a day. It's hard to keep . . . sounding convinced about it . . . Obviously, we're spending all day working on this issue, but it's hard to make it sound like you're not repeating a piece of paper." In general, the standardization of the Script and the Project's insistence that all canvassers—both rookies and veterans—practice it every day for an hour in role-playing exercises before going out to canvass was exasperating for many of the longer-term canvassers.

Although some lauded the training as ideal and "top-notch" (Larissa, 20, Portland canvass), most were uncomfortable with it. They remembered feeling ill-prepared to speak with people about the campaign. Almost 15 percent of the 2003 summer canvassers volunteered the opinion that the training period was too short. Their views were summarized by Lee, who had been working as a canvasser and a trainer out of the Portland office for about a month: "Before you go out on your first day, I personally don't believe that you get as much training as you need . . . Every new person I've worked with has felt uncomfortable when they first go out there." A number of the canvassers even described the organization's training process as a trial-by-fire. In fact, during my interviews with five different canvassers around the country, they all used those *exact* words.

Many canvassers thought they had received too little information about the People's Project before being sent out to fundraise. Having canvassed for ten weeks in the summer of 2003, Susie, the college junior I had first seen dancing on the table during the announcements in Portland, looked back on her experience in 2004:

> [By the end,] I felt like I had more questions about the organization than I did when I came in, and I didn't feel comfortable canvassing and asking people to donate money. It was something that . . . I wasn't totally 100 percent about . . . They didn't give the new canvassers a really thorough background in the organization and what they do and how they operate, and so it's kind of like, as you go out into the community and explore and talk to people, then you start learning things . . . [and] I could sympathize with the people who didn't feel comfortable with the People's Project.

Other canvassers felt the same way. During our follow-up interview in 2004, Brooks from the Portland canvass reflected: "I just don't like to campaign for something that I don't know the ins and outs about . . . [I find it] a little disconcerting."

In addition to their perceived lack of information about the organization, many canvassers found the training wanting in information about the issues for which they were fundraising. Tarun, a college graduate who had trained many canvassers in the Portland office during his four months there, pointed out: "The issues are definitely not discussed at all on the first day." Another canvasser who had been working for over a month in the Boulder office, Angel, complained: "They kind of just threw us out there without really teaching us." With so much of the training process devoted to learning the Script and how to deliver it, it is not particularly surprising that canvassers found their training about the organization and the issues lacking. In fact, during my interviews with canvassers around the country in 2003, some recited incorrect information about the organization and the campaigns for which they were recruiting members.

Although canvassers in some of the offices said they received briefings from the organization's lobbyists or from policymakers, these events happened infrequently.[3] With the average life of a canvasser being less than a month, however, most of the young people who were recruiting members on any given day understandably had limited background knowledge about the issues. Canvassers around the country said their offices did have campaign binders they could look at that provided some background with "like four or five pages of . . . just facts that we can have and then it goes more into depth" (Kendall, 21, Portland canvass). The binders also held brochures published by the research arm of the People's Project, or what Jerry from the organization's national office had called "the think tank for the [People's Project] . . . [It does] a lot of reports on behalf of the organization . . . [as]research backup." But canvassers said the binder information lacked depth and included no literature from nonpartisan scientific bodies. According to Ann, a core canvasser in the Portland office who had been reading the binder the day she spoke with me and held it on her lap during our meeting: "That's all that we have . . . There's stuff in here about what we helped do before, but it's just as vague." In addition, canvassers recalled not being introduced to any of the limited information that was in the binder until after their training period.

The majority of canvassers reported feeling most at ease canvassing on issues they already knew something about. For example, Alyssa, an Ivy League graduate who worked for the Portland canvass for six weeks, remembered drawing on her personal knowledge while canvassing for the benefit of impoverished children: "I got questions this summer . . . and, in order to answer them, I had to draw on information that I had learned elsewhere, other than what had been given to me in training sessions. It was good that I did know those things, but I don't think I could do that for environmental issues, just because I'm not well enough educated about them." Kimberly, who had just finished her junior year of college before starting at the Baltimore canvass, added: "I didn't really feel there was enough education. I knew what I was talking about because I was a political science major ... [But canvassers] do not get educated enough during training on the issue."

To make up for the lack of information provided in the organization's training, some canvassers reported trying to take this perceived problem into their own hands. However, these attempts by those the People's Project calls the "frontline of the campaign" (Kevin, 27, Portland), were not well received. Doug, a 19-year-old sophomore from Michigan who had worked for the Ann Arbor canvass during most of summer 2003, reflected:

> One of the problems on the canvass . . . was [a lack of] political education . . . [Many canvassers] couldn't dialogue about the issues, so there was this constant pressure from people to spend more time in the office on education about issues [before our daily announcements] as opposed to drilling canvassing tactics. That never happened to most people's satisfaction and . . . [we got the message] that it was not [the canvassers'] place to make those suggestions and decisions, and that it was [our] place to be directed. Pretty much, political action . . . was directed by two places: either the national office . . . or the two lobbyists for [the state branch of the organization] and it was at their discretion and their direction that people were able to take political action.

Top-down directives such as the one that Doug reported were very common and are a central component of the scripted and institutionalized setting of the canvass office.

Running the Office in a Standardized Way

Beyond the training process for new canvassers, canvass offices are run according to a clearly specified model. This experience is managed by the national office of the People's Project to maintain consistency and control over the grassroots campaigns. Because canvassing is challenging work and the offices have a high turnover rate, canvass directors are instructed to identify canvassers with potential very early on. People at all administrative levels told me how they identified people with promise. Harland, who had directed a canvass office in the Midwest before moving to Portland, described the process: The People's Project has "whittled it down to a set of pretty good basics . . . the idea is [that] if you have someone who had quote/unquote 'leadership potential,' you shove them into field managing as soon as you can." Brandon, who canvassed in the summer of 2002, told me what happened to him:

> I got thrown into a lot of things pretty much really quickly. My very next day they asked me to come in early and they had me get ready to field manage. It was pretty ridiculous. Maybe it was my second day at work . . . Then, I started canvassing awfully, so it was sort of depressing . . . and they pretty much just kept throwing us in, not really giving us a lot of direction actually.

Although Brandon expressed discomfort with his quick promotion, he thrived in the environment and chose to return to the canvass in 2003 as a director in the Atlanta office. Kimberly from the Baltimore canvass had a similar experience: "Like from day one, I knew I was training to be a field manager, they told me that on the first day . . . They said that they thought I had a lot of character or something." More than 15 percent of the canvassers from the 2003 cohort recalled being identified as having "leadership potential" and quickly becoming canvasser trainers or field managers.[4] Some began training new canvassers as early as their third day on staff. Many reported that the directors had personally told them they had leadership potential, complimenting their character, personality, charisma, or personal drive to motivate them to take on the additional work.

One of the main reasons the organization quickly tries to identify potential in its new canvassers is to get them invested in the job and the organization and make it harder for them to quit. The goal is to "solidify that level of commitment early on, [it's] sort of trial-by-fire" (Harland, 26, Portland canvass). Other tactics were also used to promote canvasser commitment to the cause. Dan, for example, recalled getting guilt from his friend, who was the director of the San Diego office, when he thought about leaving the office to take a teaching job:

> One of the reasons why I didn't leave after I immediately got that [teaching job] . . . was because my director did a great job of really making me

think . . . you can't leave because we need you. [She said,] "You play this really important role for me personally." I really liked my director a lot and I felt, if I was going to leave . . . I was putting a lot of extra stress and work on her, a friend.

When I followed up with Dan in 2004, he had given up on becoming a teacher and had chosen to continue working for the People's Project as a canvass director in California. Similar tactics were reported in the Portland office, where Tiffany said that one of the directors convinced her to canvass when she was feeling apprehensive: "They kind of tug on your heart strings and they get you to do it."

Beyond pressure from canvass directors who appealed to the personal commitment of the individual canvassers, these young people came to feel a part of the constructed canvasser community, an outcome that was promoted and cultivated by the People's Project. Canvass offices are designed to maintain an atmosphere that is contagious. The director's job is to keep excitement up and help develop a community of activists. New canvassers draw energy from their peers. With so many committed young people in a room rallying each other through chants and cheers, it is easy to become more involved. Although few of them knew any of their fellow workers before joining the canvass, they quickly became friends. Steve, an undergraduate from California, explained that, although the money and the work drew him in, it was the community that made him stay:

> I actually don't even care about the money now. My goal was just to get $1,500 because I needed a computer and I needed to buy a bed and stuff for going back to school, but . . . I already made that in my first two paychecks so . . . I'm just here because I want to do this. I mean, the people here are so inspiring, they're so positive and I don't know, I really look forward to going to work every day.

After working for the entirety of summer 2003, Steve returned to canvass out of the Portland office during his winter break, as well as in the summer of 2004.

This instant community provided by the canvass was particularly useful for college students who were only in town for the summer. In the words of Emily, who went to school out of town and was working for the Portland canvass during the summer before her junior year in college: "It's a great summer job and everyone you're working with is in a similar age group. I mean, everybody is motivated about the same things, and this is definitely the best working environment I've ever had as far as the people I work with goes . . . Everybody is really real and honest."

The canvass office is designed and managed to maintain a sense of community. Office walls are covered with quotes by famous progressive activists, including Saul Alinsky and Ralph Nader. After I remarked that the quotes were similar in offices around the country, a canvass director told me that the People's Project provides them as part of its office start-up package.

Daily announcements publicize the canvass office's social events for the week. On any given day, the office plans a pizza night or a get-together with a canvass office in a nearby area, which canvassers are expected to attend. With this type of perpetual socializing, members of the canvass office quickly make friends. Some long-term canvassers considered the organized socializing to be a mainstay of the recruitment process: "Behind closed doors, my first director's recruitment philosophy was: get them laid, get them drunk, and get them on the street" (Harland, 26, Portland canvass). At the same time, those who had personal lives outside the office were severely limited in their free time. And some canvassers' personal relationships—with partners, family members, and friends—suffered. Mike, who had worked for the Atlanta office for almost three years, reported, "I'm married and I went two and a half years without seeing my wife during the week awake more than maybe an hour or two." Since quitting in 2004 to work a more regular schedule at a music magazine, Mike declared: "Now that I've got this new job . . . I have probably literally spent more quality time with my wife in the last month than I had in the previous year."

The canvass makes no secret of its expectations for the season. Each canvass office had posted fundraising and membership targets on the walls of its "common rooms," some colorfully decorated with sparkles or streamers. Some canvass offices had novel ways of displaying their progress toward fundraising goals. Images of thermometers, growing trees, and simple bar charts adorn the walls. In the Atlanta office, where canvassers were working on a clean water campaign, any canvasser who brought in more than a specified amount of money on a given night was awarded a paper fish with his or her name on it. The canvasser was presented with the fish during announcements and was expected to affix it to a wall of the office on which a painted river had been filling with fish during the months of the campaign.

In Baltimore, the office took to collecting bricks, which canvassers added, one at a time, to their homemade wall for every $1,000 collected for their alternative energy campaign. The canvasser who raised the most money on the night the office reached the target was given the honor of adding another brick to the wall. One day in the Baltimore office, the canvass director appealed to the canvassers in the office to look for more bricks while they were out canvassing because they were running out of construction materials for their makeshift wall. Although these activities were meant to maintain a festive environment in the offices, many canvassers around the country reported feeling stressed-out by this aspect of the daily announcements. Tarun in the Portland office said: "That's a large chunk of our announcements, how much money we raise . . . so I think everyone feels that pressure to some degree or another."

Besides meeting the monetary quotas, these young people must also gather signatures on petitions and get voters to sign their names to postcards that will be mailed to policymakers. Brooks, who spent the summer between his first and second years of college working for the Portland canvass, recalled working on the postcards:

> We had a quota . . . What matters is you have these ten postcards that are all identical, that are already filled out, [and people] just sign on to it. That's the sort of thing that gets me a little bit bitter. I don't like that kind of thoughtlessness . . . They would say "OK, everybody meet back here at the bus station at the end of this time and have ten postcards filled out." . . . It doesn't matter if some Joe Schmo didn't have any idea about the subject . . . It's this idea about pressuring the state government and if somebody doesn't know anything about the subject and yet fills out this postcard then that's [the Project's] success.

Brooks found that he and his fellow canvassers were serving an instrumental purpose in what Elizabeth Clemens calls "means-ends schemas."[5] The People's Project was using the canvassers to accumulate political clout in the form of postcards to bolster its lobbying efforts on their clean water campaign. Instead of educating the public about ways to pressure their political representatives personally, or actually cleaning up the polluted river—both of which are difficult, long-term projects—the organization identified how much money and how many names it needed to work the political system and then paid the canvassers to achieve these instrumental goals.

In addition to broadcasting the successes of particular canvassers and the office's progress toward achieving the campaign's goals, directors emphasized the importance of running inspirational announcements for both the new and older canvassers. In the words of Harland: "Right away, you're in this really fun place with people your age who are just incredibly psyched to get out there and have doors slammed in [their] faces . . . I think often enough you can judge the [monetary] average on a given day by how crazy the announcements were." This "craziness" can involve what Paul-Brian and I had observed in the Portland office, including singing, chanting, and cheering for new canvassers before they went out on their first days.

In the Boulder office, the daily announcements ended with all of the canvassers huddled around a small wooden statue of a fisherman. On the count of three, everyone cheered "This is what democracy looks like," and the crews dispersed to the streets for the day's canvassing. During that summer, I observed canvassers around the country becoming visibly caught up in the rapture of the daily announcements, chanting and cheering along with their leaders. Although I was unable to verify any direct correlation between the more exhilarating announcements and the success of a particular day, I did notice that more people—both existing canvassers and trainees—seemed to come back to canvass on the days after a particularly inspiring announcement session.

Even though motivational announcements were a key tool for maintaining the community of canvassers, some reported being uncomfortable with this aspect of the job. Marie, who had worked for five weeks in the

Ann Arbor office, had very strong feelings about the daily announcements: "I felt there was ... a lot of phoniness ... [including the] general campiness of saying a cheer before you go out [to canvass], which, you know, it's kind of corny but whatever, you deal with it." Marie was disturbed by what she perceived as the insincerity of the office setting and reported that it contributed to her decision to leave the canvass after six weeks.

Like the office procedures, the politics of the canvass itself are also centralized. All of the campaign goals were set for each canvassing office by the regional or national branches of the People's Project. Jason, a college graduate who was working as one of the many directors in the Portland office, discussed the origin of their campaign goals: "It trickles down from [the] national [office], I think to regional, then per office ... Those are also based on the projections of what we should have in terms of team size, so they already know, before the season even starts how big we're supposed to get, and they make their calculations on what they can produce from that." As a canvasser who did not hold an administrative position, Tiffany had a different perspective. She recalled speaking with the directors about her concerns regarding a campaign: "In the Portland office ... it wasn't a really truly democratic workplace ... [I would] talk to them about it, but it won't necessarily affect [anything], you know, you can talk to them about [the campaign], but they still have to follow these policies that are coming down [from above] . . . whether or not they agree with them." In other words, Tiffany recognized that the directors were only doing their jobs, following orders that had come from the national and regional offices.

Outside of their day-to-day work, canvassers are expected to participate in numerous political activities that are also scripted by the organization. When the national or regional office decides to hold a press conference, for example, canvassers are supposed to attend and show their spirit. In one case, canvassers in the Portland office dressed up as fishermen for a press conference. And as I described in Chapter 1, members of the Atlanta canvass came out to hold chainsaws (most of which they were unable to start) during a nationally coordinated chainsaw salute to protest the Bush administration's forest policies. Also, canvassers were sometimes asked to come in early to write letters to politicians or opinion pieces to be submitted to local newspapers. In both of these cases, the People's Project provided the canvassers with sample text to use as a model. Although all of these activities took place outside normal canvassing time, none of them involved monetary compensation.

These sorts of top-down practices made many canvassers feel that they had no autonomy. According to Doug, who had canvassed in Ann Arbor after his sophomore year in college: "The canvassers and field managers really had no say in the overall direction of where the campaign was going and in terms of politics, we sort of just marched around and did what the upper two levels told us to, and further we had . . . very little say in how the canvass would go." Some canvassers felt alienated by the centralization of the campaigns. Many canvassers even thought that it seriously limited the ways in which the organization's members, as well as the canvassers themselves, could engage politically. Doug continued: "There is no accountability from the membership to the leadership and . . . there are very few attempts on the part of leadership to leverage that membership into more directed political power." With so many canvassers working as paid activists around the country, canvassers like Doug saw opportunities for political mobilization that involved rallying the thousands of members to do more than write checks, but the organization did not support such member-based work.

Canvassers were not encouraged to express their own personal politics in individually motivated ways. Instead, they were given very clear signals from the organization about how to engage and when. A handful of the summer 2003 canvassers found their personal politics to be more left-leaning than those of the organization. Although they had joined the People's Project to earn a living while furthering causes they believed in, after working at the canvass office many became bothered by its focus on money and fundraising. In addition, they started to feel as if their opinions and political ideals did not matter to the organization. Some canvassers even became concerned about the Project's mainstream tactics and attempts to change the system from within. A number expressed disappointment in the organization's institutional goals and decided to leave.

Also, time on the beat can be disheartening, with so many doors slammed and donations denied. But the canvass office is designed to be an exciting environment, which enables some canvassers to tune out the negative in favor of the positive, at least for a time. Joanne, who worked for the Boulder canvass between her sophomore and junior years at a progressive college on the East Coast, for example, found that even though her politics and those of the canvass were not a perfect match, her work made enough of a difference to be worth her time: "I mean a revolution would be great . . . [But] I still feel like it's important that we do this, and [urban sprawl] is an important issue too. While it's one of many, at this point, I still feel like every little bit does help and the more we can get things moving in the right direction, the better off we'll be." Erin, 20, made similar points. Despite having lost faith in the political process that the People's Project attempted to work, she returned to canvass out of the San Diego office five summers in a row. Here, Erin rationalizes her decision to keep working as a canvasser for the Project:

My politics have changed . . . I have a lot less faith in lobbying and like traditional . . . politics than I used to. So, I don't necessarily . . . support [lobbying], as far as getting things accomplished. [But] canvassing is a really good way to do that regardless of what your belief is . . . I basically identify as an anarchist so . . . electoral politics and . . . the representative government that we don't really have, I don't really see much validity in that.

In 2004, Erin reported being involved in a number of different social movement organizations, many of which employed direct action tactics, such as civil disobedience, to achieve their goals.

The central coordination of the local grassroots offices of the People's Project extended to the organization's employment policies. A number of canvassers expressed frustration with the Project's procedures for firing people. Although all canvassers were aware that they had to maintain quota to stay on staff, they reported mysterious firings that were unexplained by the directors. These experiences were particularly difficult because people's departures broke up a community of friends. One undergraduate at a progressive liberal arts college who had been working at the Baltimore canvass for the majority of summer 2003, Kay, recalled the circumstances under which she decided to leave:

> When I left, the campaign was pretty much degenerated. They had gotten a new director and he had fired some of my friends so there was a lot of tension between the field managers . . . and the director . . . They were like, "Oh let's raise $10,000 to meet a certain goal." I just said, "I don't care, I've really done enough campaigning and I can't keep working twelve hours a day," so I quit.

Canvassers provided numerous accounts of staff purges. Marie, a recent college graduate, said that, in the Ann Arbor office, staff members just returned to the office one day to find their friends gone:

> I felt there was a lot of secrecy going on . . . not telling people the full truth of where people went when they disappeared, you know, not telling the truth of what happened to them, and that kind of got on my nerves a lot. So, I didn't feel I was fully respected as a member of that office. I felt like I was a pretty much expendable person who was just useful for bringing in money . . . I felt like I could have offered more and I could have gotten more if people were just more honest with each other there.

These unexplained firings clearly affected the morale of the canvassers, and a number of the young people from the summer of 2003 left the canvass with bitterness.

Many canvassers complained about the organization's overall employment policies, which were set by the national office and based on monetary quotas and a commission-based pay system. Canvassers pointed out the inconsistency of the Project's politics: it promoted a left-leaning political agenda but did not practice progressive labor policies. Cheri summed up many of the canvassers feelings: "I think it's kind of hypocritical for [the People's Project] to be . . . [a] progressive organization but their labor policies aren't very good."

Another member of the Portland canvass, Tiffany, who worked there for nine months in 2003, explained:

> They're supposed to be trying to do good things, like they're not looking

at a whole picture . . . You have to carry on the labor side of things too, you know you can't treat your employees like peons . . . Sometimes, it worked out to less than minimum wage honestly with the hours that you put in, because you're not paid an hourly wage in the first place. You're paid base pay plus bonuses for whatever over quota you get [when canvassing]. But that totally doesn't have anything to do with the fact that they want people to come in[to] . . . the office two hours before you start canvassing . . . and, oftentimes, they really want people to come in and help run the office and it's strictly volunteer. Like, if you're coming in and training the new people or running role-plays with them and everything, you're just doing that to help out.

Higher-ups in the organization confirmed that canvassers' wages were low, but they had a very different perspective on canvasser pay. One regional director pointed out that the People's Project considered canvasser commitment to be inversely proportionate to their pay. In other words, door-to-door canvassers, who made the least money for the most time commitment and tended to earn a smaller paycheck than their street canvassing counterparts, were considered to be more serious activists by the organization.

Such a counterintuitive perspective on the relationship between earnings and personal commitment may have contributed to the Project's labor practices. In more than one interview, canvassers mentioned the organization's history of labor problems.[6] In the words of Thomas, a 20-year-old field manager who had just finished his junior year in college: "I heard the [People's Project] actually doesn't have a great policy on unions." Canvassers' complaints were consistent with stories about the Project's response to efforts to unionize specific canvass offices. A 2002 article in *LA Weekly* publicized what may be the most well documented case. After the directors "lodged a complaint with the state labor board and informed their bosses they wanted to form a union, they quickly found themselves out of work."[7] About the same case, the *Student Underground*[8] wrote that workers in a California office "reported to work one day to find the office closed—permanently." The staff there believes the office was closed because its staff was trying to unionize. Two directors at the office had advocated the union because they were having trouble getting reimbursement from the national office for supplies, and they hadn't received the health insurance they had been promised. Also, workers felt that they weren't making a livable wage.[9] Although identical union-busting tactics have been employed by corporations like Wal-Mart, I was surprised to hear such vitriolic accounts of a progressive national group by its own workers.[10] By the time I followed up with this cohort of canvassers in 2004, many had become disillusioned with the organization's canvassing process. When I asked whether they would consider canvassing again, many reported that they would, but not for the People's Project.

Managing the Directors

The unintended consequences of the centralized management of the canvass also affected the directors of these grassroots offices. Although working as a canvasser involves long hours and difficult work, and canvass directors only canvass an average of three days a week, their jobs are much more demanding.

Stephanie, a long-term canvasser, declared that she made significantly more money than the directors in the Atlanta office because her salary was based on commission, and for that reason she had never sought a promotion: "[Canvass directors] were pushed past the limit in terms of, you know, things being difficult . . . even things like their pay . . . [They] were the ones who had to either make everybody else round up money and chip in to pay [for social events], and then get paid back two or three weeks later." Canvassers and canvass directors alike reported the directors working about eighty hours a week during the summer canvass, and sixty to sixty-five hours a week during the rest of the year,[11] for which they received very little financial compensation.

Lori, who had directed a canvass office in California for nine months, explained the perspective of many of her fellow directors: "For those of us who [were] more disenchanted, I'd say we definitely . . . felt like we were being taken advantage of." Canvass directors even reported having to work seven days a week at times to support weekend canvasses, camping canvasses, and canvasses at concerts, festivals, and other special events. At least one director was required to work at all canvassing events. In addition, field managers in some offices reported being expected to participate in *leadership training* meetings on Sundays. Lori continued:

> On top of working . . . an enormous amount of hours . . . it's not really clock-in, clock-out, because if there's any kind of training during the weekend or if there's any kind of campaign action, basically you're on call unless you can come up with a really good excuse. So, there really wasn't much respect for personal life . . . We did everything on budget . . . [and] there is an expectation of, for instance, if people fly in from out of town for some reason, you're sort of expected to shuttle them back and forth to the airport, and put them up in your personal home.

Because directors worked such long hours, were expected to house visiting out-of-towners, and had to cover the expenses for many of the group's activities out of their own pockets, many canvass directors left the People's Project before fulfilling their contracts.

Lori explained the events leading up to her departure: "We had a meeting in Portland and they didn't have the money to reimburse folks for gas, food, or anything. For those of us driving up from San Diego, [it] was expensive . . . [It was a] pretty major trip and we stopped different places and worked and canvassed on the way up, but . . . it was just ridiculous and I felt that there were some things that were exploitive of [our] idealism!" Canvassers from several offices reported that directors quit because they got "stressed out and couldn't handle it" (Mike, 33, Atlanta canvass).[12] In fact, only about 45 percent of the directors I met around the country in the summer of 2003 were still working for the People's Project in 2004.[13]

Lori shared her personal observations about director attrition: "Of all the people who were hired . . . [as canvass directors and assistant canvass directors] in California, over half of them quit earlier than they said they would . . . I looked at a directory . . . and I remembered, you know, there are eighteen names there for people who were hired as directors or assistant directors, and I know that by the time I left, ten of them had also left." This college graduate, who had worked in soup kitchens and on multiple political issues since she was a teenager, had come to the job to put her idealism to work. When I met her initially in summer 2003, she told me she intended to work in the nonprofit sector for the rest of her life. By the summer of 2004, however, she had left her canvass director's job early and was taking some time off before going back to school to pursue a law degree. After her experience with the canvass, she said her interests had been directed away from politics and she was more attracted to service-oriented work.

Although many canvass directors were hired into programs for college graduates that required them to direct canvass offices during the summer months, some canvass directors had moved up after working as canvassers. Approximately half of the canvass directors in the 2003 cohort had been promoted internally. A few people observed that the organization seemed to have a mold that they expected directors to fit. Harland shared his observations from having worked with the People's Project in two canvass offices over more than three years: "The people . . . that advance in [the Project] are the ones who have proven themselves to be flexible and willing to kind of take one for the team." If they did not fit the mold, these young people had a hard time. Mike, for example, recalled applying for a number of director positions during his two years canvassing for the People's Project: "I have applied for several jobs, have not gotten them, and I have a general feeling that folks in the [Project] just think maybe I'm a little too outside of the mold or outside of the box for them." Even when the Atlanta office director quit at the last minute, he was not offered the job: "I applied for the job here in Atlanta. Didn't get it. The person who got it was somebody that I had trained who had been here not as long as me. She quit after two weeks . . . Then, I ran the office pretty much just by default for two months until they found another director, and they never once even suggested or offered to me that I might, perhaps, be[come] the director."

The only director position that Mike was ever offered by the People's Project was in Tampa Bay, Florida, where, for personal reasons, he was unable to move. This job offer is consistent with the accounts of other canvass directors who told me that the structure of the organization is designed to keep canvass directors on the move. Mike explained that his unwillingness to move may have affected his future job opportunities with the organization: "I grew up in Georgia, I've lived here for over twenty years, my wife is from Georgia, [and] all of our friends are here. This is where I want to live, and I'm not going to move and that has definitely been an obstacle."

Although some directors reported that the People's Project respected the wishes of the "people who are married and have families" (Rebecca, 22, San Diego canvass), many referred to the organization's policy of "geoflexibility." Canvass directors are expected to be almost rootless and both able and willing to move around. Having directed a canvass office in the Midwest, Harland explained the organization's rationale: "Directing demands a lot of your time and if you're moved from Point A to Point B, you don't have roots, so putting in twelve to fourteen hours a day isn't quite as bad [and] you don't have friends to remind you that you're a lunatic . . . The positive aspect [of moving around] is that you're allowed to immerse yourself that much [more] in the work . . . If it doesn't drive you completely insane then you'll fall in love with it."

Most of the canvass directors I met in the summer of 2003 had relocated for the job and understood that it was a necessary component of work in progressive politics. Laurena, who had recently been promoted to canvass director after canvassing for six months in Boulder, was expecting a move in a few weeks. She recalled being informed that she would be moving to either Oregon, Arizona, or New York. When I met with Jessica, who was running the Baltimore office in 2003, she had moved there only a month earlier to start the campaign. Having directed an office in the Midwest the previous summer, she was unfamiliar with Baltimore and had only recently discovered her local supermarket.

Although the practice of geoflexibility may make sense to an organization that is constantly responding to campaign needs and changes in its staff, from a political perspective the rationale is less convincing. How can the People's Project run effective *grassroots* campaigns that are coordinated by rootless workaholics? By hiring geoflexible young people who are not grounded in the localities and places where they are working, this strategy can be counterproductive. For example, there are many potential benefits to be had from Mike's local knowledge of Atlanta, which he gained from more than twenty years of living and working there. It is these kinds of personal connections within communities that Robert Putnam is referring to when he writes about social capital.[14]

Instead of connecting canvass offices to preexisting local progressive institutions through its canvass directors, the People's Project chooses to move them around regularly. As a direct result, the canvass directors' personal bonds with people in the communities and their connections to local organizations that might be sympathetic partners for their grassroots campaigns are severely limited. In fact, when I asked the canvass directors if they participated in any local political or civic work outside of their jobs, most laughed, pointing out that they barely had time to sleep or do their laundry, let alone volunteer or attend community meetings.

By capitalizing on its employees' idealism and desire to work in progressive politics in America, the People's Project has developed a system that maximizes the work that it can get out of its young administrators. Although there is nothing wrong with getting the most out of young people who have chosen to make a difference by working in grassroots political campaigns, there are significant unintended consequences to the lives of the individual directors. In addition, this system is having a significant effect on progressive politics in America more broadly.

Chapter 3

Making a Difference as a Canvasser

Jobs with a Conscience

I t was a hot and sunny week in July 2003 when I met the canvassers in Boulder, Colorado. Over soy lattes and echinacea-infused fruit smoothies, they related the stories of how they came to work for what posters and websites had called "jobs with a conscience" at a grassroots campaign office of the People's Project. Some had recently moved to Boulder, others were students at the University of Colorado in town, but many just stumbled onto the job.

One such canvasser was Peter, a 21-year-old junior from a university in North Carolina, who said: "Yeah, I just randomly decided with a couple friends that I was going to come out here and I had looked for an internship, and the place that I was looking ended up not hiring." He continued, "So, I just decided I'd come out anyway and look for a job and came across this and figured . , it's a good cause." Another recent transplant, John, a 19-year-old from St. Louis, literally happened upon the work. While job-hunting on Pearl Street, he was stopped by a canvasser. Although he was interested in the cause, he had no money. The canvasser suggested he apply for a job with the campaign office: "I had my interview and got the job . . . Been here ever since." Similarly, a canvasser from the campaign office in Portland, Oregon, said his car had broken down while he was following the band Phish, which had a Grateful Dead–like fan base, around the country. He decided to work for the canvass just until he could afford to repair the car and get back on the road.

Although some of the canvassers, like Peter and John, just stumbled onto the job, others had applied to work at the People's Project on their college campuses. For them, working on these grassroots campaigns was a way to make a difference and apply to the real world what they had learned in political science classes. Shiv, for example, had recently graduated from a liberal arts college in the Northwest. He recounted: "On my school campus, people from this office came and were searching for workers for the summer. I definitely needed a job for the summer and it was interesting too 'cause I definitely want to be a little bit more proactive in what I do." Beyond those who learned about the job from the Project's fliers stapled to bulletin boards and lampposts on campus, a number of canvassers came to the Project through websites such as summerjobs.com and idealist.org, which aims to connect "people, organizations and resources to help build a world where all people can live free and dignified lives."[1]

Although each canvasser came to the People's Project with a different story, once they started their jobs, their individual stories converged into a single shared experience. This convergence is a direct result of the standardized model for grassroots organizing employed by the People's Project. To illustrate this point, I introduce many canvassers in this chapter. While it may be hard to keep them all straight, what is important to note is that these individuals, whose personal histories had motivated them to "make a difference," had identical experiences working at the Project's offices around the country.[2] In many instances, however, these experiences were not what the canvassers had expected.

Why Do They Join?

Many canvassers joined "to make a difference." The canvass provides young people with an opportunity to express their political leanings and get paid for their work; it is an alternative to the typical boring summer jobs: waiting tables, lifeguarding, working at Starbucks. Most of the canvassers were drawn to the idea of making a difference *while* earning money. As George, a University of Colorado freshman working at the Boulder office, explained: "I needed a summer job, but beyond that, I was just looking for something that would be worthwhile on another level, you know, other than just something that earns money, and I've had a definite interest and passion for environmentalism for a long time but haven't really been able to get fully involved . . . at school."

Kelly, a 19-year-old who had just finished her first year of college, had similar motivations for joining the People's Project:

Basically, I moved from Maine, which is where I go to school . . . [My roommate and I came] on a whim: let's go to Portland, we'll be able to find jobs . . . So, when we got here, we did the whole job search thing . . . We were just going to waitress . . . and the thought definitely came up [about] selling our eggs, which was ix-nayed because, you know . . . I saw a little snippet in the paper, and it looked like a great opportunity to actually get involved and have a meaningful summer. So, that's basically why I'm [here] . . . It was totally personal and that's how I got reflecting . . . It was never about the money or making the commission. Even though, I mean, that's obviously a plus of this job but that's not why anybody's here honestly. I mean, if you wanted to make money, you would definitely be doing something different.

For other canvassers, joining the canvass was an extension of their personal interests. Dawn, a 24-year-old college graduate who was also working in Boulder, said she took the job after taking classes in environmental studies at school: "I figured it was a great way to actually get involved in what I had studied. It's better than waitressing and things like that, to make more—a lot more—of a difference than some other jobs that I could be doing."

Some canvassers' family politics motivated them to work for the canvass. Almost 15 percent of the canvassers described coming from political families. Two of the canvassers reported that their parents were involved in local politics. Some came from families with parents who were die-hard Democrats with "like ten campaign signs out in the front yard for every single election" (Kathy, 25, Portland canvass). Caleb, a canvasser from the Atlanta office, recalled his mother's work for the Green Party: "She drove [Ralph] Nader whenever he was in town, in our family car, and that was kind of cool." Both of Bruce's parents were active union members. The 19-year-old sophomore from the Midwest who was working at the Ann Arbor canvass explained: "My father was in some unions in Detroit and my mother has been part of the UAW [United Automobile, Aerospace and Agricultural Implement Workers of America] and a lot of other big unions . . . I've grown up in a very liberal and very organized political household and doing this kind of thing, I guess, is right up the alley that they would support and kind of what they instilled in me as I grew up."

On the other hand, there were also canvassers who participated *despite* the wishes of their families. Although some of them admitted that their parents weren't completely happy about their job choices, others said their work on the canvass had changed their parents' minds. For example, Lisa, a 26-year-old college graduate from the Northeast, spoke to me after she had been directing campaign offices on the West Coast for three years. She recalled how her job had transformed her father:

> My experience growing up was that my dad always used to yell at canvassers when they came to the house . . . He was really disappointed to find out that I was canvassing . . . [and] he tried really hard to get me to do something else. My parents actually used to send me, like, "how-to-find-a-job" books even after I had started . . . canvass directing . . . But then I got him to the point where he decided he wasn't going to yell at people anymore when they came to the door, which was really nice. And then, two summers ago, he called me up and he said, "Hey, you'd be really proud of me. Somebody came to the door and she started talking, and I told her to stop talking and that you worked for the same people and that I was going to give her money. So I gave her money, so I'm a member now." . . . [More recently,] he's actually constantly asking me what we're working on and stuff like that, and what he can do about it, which is kind of cool.

Young people joined the canvass to make a difference, as an extension of their interests, and in response to their families. Most of the canvassers were politically progressive, but had yet to get involved in politics; only about a quarter mentioned having any type of political or environmental experience before starting their work with the People's Project. Although most had not been politically active until then, the canvassers were much more knowledgeable about the American political process and were significantly more civic-minded than the population as a whole.[3] For example, they knew how the political system worked and about Americorps, the "network of national service programs" that was started during the Clinton administration.[4] These young people also read the newspaper and talked about politics significantly more than their noncanvassing counterparts. (For a detailed comparison between the canvassers and the national sample see the Appendix.) The average age of the canvassers was 22, and 60 percent of them were currently enrolled in school; however, very few reported participating in political or civic activities on campus. For most canvassers, working for the People's Project was their first real attempt to engage civically or politically. Their work for the Project's grassroots campaigns constituted their formative political experiences in progressive politics and therefore had the potential to leave a lasting impression.

Why Do They Stay?

These politically aware young people joined the campaign to make a difference; and while they were working for the People's Project they genuinely felt as if they did. Almost all of the canvassers I interviewed during the summer of 2003 wore their idealism on their sleeves: they believed they were helping to change the world. Many told me about their individual successes and contributions to the organization.

Jessica, a 24-year-old graduate of an Ivy League school, who was one of the directors of the Baltimore office for the summer, explained: "I'm a fundraiser so I'm making a lot of money for [the People's Project], which is what they need to have . . . people working on these issues . . . I'll probably end up raising like $6,000 this summer, so that's good and I feel like I'm making a difference. I mean that's a small part of someone's salary." A representative from the Project's national office outlined three main goals for the canvass: "To help build the organizations that we canvas for . . . their resources, learning and members . . . to help [these groups] win their campaigns . . . [and] to train a ton of activists." A number of canvassers mentioned these same reasons for canvassing. But most canvassers, like Jessica, focused on the amount of money they brought in as their personal indicator of success.

Jessica's attention to the money is not particularly surprising given the organization's emphasis on monetary quotas. Once a trainee raises what is determined to be the quota for a particular office and/or campaign, he or she is hired as a member of the staff. Even after trainees become staff members, however, they are still held to monetary targets; canvassers who do not make quota are asked to leave. Canvassers reported that the amount of time they were given before being fired was arbitrarily determined by the directors of each office. Most stated that they needed to meet the average quota over the week to stay on staff. Others, however, recounted stories of being told that they could stay on because of their personal connections or their "potential." One such canvasser was Sarah, whose housemate and best friend was a director in the Portland office. She reported that her relationship with the director helped her during the few weeks that she did not earn quota: "If I was just some . . . random person they might have fired me at some point, but they didn't."

Salaries are also determined by a commission system that is based on how much money an individual canvasser brings in during a given week. Emily, a college sophomore who had only been working for the Portland canvass for six days, already knew she was making a difference: "If you're getting the members, you just feel like you're making more, that much more of a difference, you know, like you're actually raising money for the cause."

Although there is no doubt that these canvassers viewed fundraising as a benchmark for their success, a number of them saw their achievements as going *beyond* the money. Kevin, a 27-year-old college senior who had been working for the canvass for almost two years when I followed up with him in 2004, reported: "I probably average just over two people that I sign up a day, and I talk to anywhere from thirty to forty people a day, and so whether or not I'm raising money, I'm at least hopefully causing something to click in a few of those other thirty-some people that I speak with and, based on the interactions I have, I believe truly that I do."

Consistent with Kevin's interpretation, many of these young people felt that they were providing a much-needed service to the American public by educating them about important issues. Dan, a 23-year-old college graduate who worked for the San Diego canvass, noted:

> [The work we do is] to raise people's awareness about what's going on. A lot of people . . . want to get involved, they are happy to see you at

the door . . . They have lives to live, they have bills to pay, but when you come knocking on their door, you're giving them [an] opportunity to not only learn about what's going on, but giv[ing] them an opportunity to change that . . . I think that what the canvass does is really give people an opportunity to change things . . . They're actually making a difference [by putting] pressure on politicians. When the public is informed and knows what's going on, you know, they're a lot more likely to do something about it than if they're sitting and watching *Friends*.

These thoughts were echoed by canvassers around the country, such as Brian, a college senior who had been working in the Portland office for a month and a half. He observed: "It's a great way just to spread the word and educate people in their everyday lives [who], perhaps, don't get this information from the local news media, and don't take the time out of their lives to research on the Web what different environmental things are going on."

Most of the canvassers considered their work to be about identifying like-minded individuals. They were out there on the streets directly educating the public about issues that already concerned them, such as the pollution of local waterways, alternative energy options, or urban sprawl. Stephanie, who had been working in the Atlanta campaign office for over two years, pointed out: "I definitely make a difference . . . getting [to] the people who are already out there, who are already supportive . . . It's just like they are waiting for that opportunity." One of the directors in the Portland office added: "It's more about getting the people who are already there to . . . do something about it, rather than push people who are kind of on the fence over it" (Will, 30, Portland canvass).

Although most of the canvassers had views that were consistent with those of Stephanie and Will, some considered the act of canvassing to be about converting people. For example, Tamara, an 18-year-old who had just finished her first year at a small liberal arts college in the Northeast and had spent the past three and a half weeks canvassing for the Portland office, stated: "There are certainly people that are not converted but there *are* some and . . . it feels wonderful." In fact, one of the members of the Boulder canvass, Billy, a 19-year-old freshman at a university in the South, had come to Colorado for the summer primarily to work with a campus Christian Ministry group. He likened street canvassing to street evangelism, pointing out that the skills were very similar for both but that "the goals are obviously different."

Whether or not the canvassers felt as if they were converting people, many believed that, through their face-to-face interactions with the public, they were motivating American citizens to take action. In the words of Shannon, who had recently graduated from an Ivy League school and had moved to Baltimore to direct its canvass office in May: "Going door to door and talking to people individually, I am able to talk with them directly about environmental, political, [and] public health . . . issues, and how they individually can get involved and improve their own environment, and so it's a really effective tool in public education, getting a lot of people interested in how they can improve their own environment." Shannon and the canvassers in her office spent the majority of summer 2003 working on a campaign to pass a state law to increase alternative energy use in Maryland.

Another director, Nicole, in the San Diego canvass, had started working for the People's Project when she was an undergraduate. She spoke about the ways that canvassing generates political influence:

> I don't know how it would work otherwise . . . Surely the number of people that we talk to, I mean, in San Diego at this point in the summer we have talked to probably more than 20,000 residents. There's nobody else that I know of who is going out and talking to that many San Diego residents about any issue, so I think that that's pretty cool. And, when we meet with legislators and let them know this, I mean, it's definitely more constituents than they come in contact with.

A number of the canvassers agreed with Nicole and Shannon: through the canvass, they could effectively address political and environmental issues by giving American citizens the opportunity to engage actively in the political process. By "educating" the public, many canvassers felt as if they were practicing democracy-in-action, bridging the gap in the political process in the United States that prevented people from participating fully.

They understood that people were busy with work and other distractions. Moreover, they accepted their position as paid activists as both a privilege and a duty. Erin, a 20-year-old junior from a midwestern college who was working for the San Diego canvass for the summer, explained that canvassing was a way to bring political power to more people:

> I feel like [canvassing is] the best [way of confronting political problems]. I feel like there's such a problem with ignorance and apathy . . . I feel like the political system is kind of amorphous to a lot of people and that . . . not everyone gets to be a political activist as their job. This is a way to shift the power from the legislator to the public. So, we're going around talking to regular people, and [even] if they don't get involved, they at least know something.

Bridgette, a 21-year-old college student working as an assistant canvass director in the Portland office, asserted that the canvass provides a necessary shortcut for busy Americans: "It's a really easy way for people to actually get involved without having to do a tremendous amount of research on their own, or having to lobby themselves . . . So many people work and have absolutely no time, they have kids and bills to pay. We're just kind of like . . . [the] middleman between the lobbyists and . . . the voices of the public." Continuing, she emphasized the significance of the face-to-face interactions that canvassing offers: "We don't even have to wait for them to come to us."

Although many canvassers felt as though the American political system did not afford people the opportunity to become involved, they saw the role of the canvasser as not simply being an activist, but providing citizens with the tools to act politically by shaping the form of their participation.

Even though the canvassers alluded to the ways that their work brings politics to the people, very few said that members they had recruited actually got involved beyond making a monetary contribution. The People's Project did, however, make a few attempts to engage the organization's members. For example, David, one of the directors in the Boulder office, got local businesspeople to sign letters saying that they supported the canvass's goals for renewable energy. Similarly, Gretchen, who had been working through the organization's fellowship program for a year and had spent her summer directing the Ann Arbor office as part of her postgraduate fellowship,[5] described the ways that people could sign up to be voluntary "activists" for the People's Project: "When they either sign a postcard or sign up as a member, there's a little box . . . and it actually says 'volunteer' . . . and if they check that box, it means that we give them a call once every couple of months when there's an important vote coming up in Congress and ask them to contact their representatives."

The People's Project was also in the process of developing ways to use the Internet to mobilize these voluntary "activists." Emma, a San Diego canvass director working on that project, explained:

> [The Internet outreach is for anyone who has] signed up through the canvass office . . . [or has] given us their e-mail address, and approved our getting in touch with them on a regular basis . . . Each week we send them something . . . and ask them to help out in our work, either by doing an on-line action or by actually doing real world activities like showing up to a hearing and testifying or telling us their personal story [so] that we can use it in media events or something like that.

For most members who signed up through the canvass, however, involvement in the organization was limited to donating money and filling out postcards on the street or at the door. Such membership devoid of any real interaction or involvement at the local level has become the foundation of progressive grassroots politics in the United States today. Because most of these groups do not have local chapters where the members meet, and are made up of "very sparse networks of subnational affiliates,"[6] the meaning of "membership" has changed significantly. Even the canvassers who had become members of their own campaigns did not recall much contact beyond receiving an e-mail or two after they left. Gary, a 22-year-old college graduate who had canvassed for the Portland office for three months, reported signing up for the Human Rights Campaign while he was working as a canvasser. During a follow-up interview in the summer of 2004, I asked him if he had gone to this organization's local meetings or other events. He responded: "No, but they don't really e-mail me with meeting updates . . . I would if they would keep me informed like that."

Canvassers also stayed because they had seen their work yield political success. Even though the actual engagement with the members who were recruited through the campaign was relatively limited, a number of the canvassers pointed to specific successes, linking their actions on the ground to political outcomes at the state or national level, or both. They noted that, by becoming members, citizens gave the Project's advocates the political clout they needed to influence elected representatives. Having worked for the People's Project on and off in California for almost a year, Dan from the San Diego office reflected on the political success of particular state and national campaigns with which he had been involved. These victories included stopping the building of oil rigs off of the coast of Santa Barbara, passing a renewable energy portfolio for the state of California, and protecting the Arctic National Wildlife Refuge.[7] Many who had worked through the completion of a campaign had experienced similar successes, but they also recognized that it takes a very long time for political campaigns to work. Most canvassers never got to see the conclusion of the campaigns for which they recruited support.

When asked what determined whether a canvasser would be able to make quota and attain staff-member status, most canvassers agreed that "there's no standard . . . Joe Canvasser [who] is going to go out there and do great. It's the people who are themselves" (Dan, 23, San Diego). Nonetheless, their responses were consistent with those of Jerry from the national office. When I asked him what made a good canvasser, he replied that it was "enthusiasm" for the issues or the organization, or both, and for "getting involved in the Democratic process."

Canvassers also stayed if their personalities suited the job. Peter in the Boulder office added that personality played a big role in canvassers' success: "I think canvassing really revolves around personality and how well you're able to hold a conversation with people . . . I mean you're talking to people you've never met before on the street, and so to convince them that they should give you money could be difficult . . . That's why I think a lot of it really just has to do with how comfortable you are doing it and how comfortable you can make them feel." This gregarious young man with an interest in business ethics had just finished his junior year at an elite school back East. He remembered picking up canvassing very quickly on his first day:

> After about twenty minutes [into my training day] I heard [my trainer] do it like two or three times . . . I just thought I'd give it a shot and, actually, it went fine . . . It's really just how comfortable you are with it . . . with talking to people on the street . . . I don't find any reason to be uncomfortable talking to people. I figure if they are willing to stop, then I might as well make the best of it.

Other canvassers, however, were not as outgoing as Peter. Although they were enthusiastic about working for progressive change, many recalled feeling nervous and uncomfortable talking to strangers on their doorsteps or on the street. A few canvassers did feel that the experience helped them combat their shyness. And some of these young people described finally finding their voices through canvassing. Lee, a 19-year-old student who attended a local community college in Portland and was working for the street canvass there, thought about the role that his personality played in canvassing and the way the experience was changing him: "I've actually been an introverted person my entire life, and so this is a weird thing that I have this job now, but I'm loving it, and I'm learning how to talk to people." He also contemplated the role that personality plays in canvassing:

> It does help if you're extroverted because when you're out there in the field and talking to people, you need to be happy and bouncy even when you're not talking to somebody. If somebody sees you two blocks down and you're looking morose and you're looking at the ground, and they get within twenty feet of you, within greeting distance, and you perk up, "Oh hi, you got a minute?" They know it's fake . . . [So] I try to be happy when I'm out there in the field.

Some canvassers stayed because canvassing develops skills that can be used in the future. Canvassers who became comfortable with the experience even reported finding that the skills they developed through canvassing were useful elsewhere. Jason, for example, started working as a canvasser after a director in the Portland office knocked on his door in January 2003. By the time I met him in July, he himself had become a director there. He found that "canvassing is a skill that you bring to everything that you do." Similarly, Emma from the San Diego office who was working on the Project's Internet presence, spoke about the utility of the skills she learned canvassing:

> The more organizing I do, the more I realize everything is just a different form of canvassing. So, it's kind of like doing staff management and having conversations with people where you're trying to convince them that they should really be invested in whatever it is you're trying to get them to do, whether it's sign on to a coalition letter, or stay on staff another week, or whatever. It's the same conversation, the same exact communication skills in learning canvassing or what I use on a daily basis . . . Definitely some lobby meetings are just like . . . the same conversation you would have on somebody's doorstep.

Why Do They Leave?

Although most canvassers believed that they were personally making a difference at the People's Project, many did not stay at the job for very long. Canvassing is predominantly summer work. The People's Project runs many of its grassroots campaigns out of temporary offices during the summer months. Over half of the canvassers were working for the Project during their summer vacations from college, and about 15 percent reported returning to school as their main reason for leaving.

As part of the initial interview in summer 2003, I asked all of the canvassers how they intended to continue their political and environmental activities after the summer. Almost 100 percent of them told me that canvassing had given them a chance to participate in the political process on a regular basis, not just during elections, and that they intended to stay involved in politics after the summer. And most of them followed through: within the year, 95 percent of them had written or telephoned an editor or a public official, or had signed a petition about issues that concerned them; 79 percent had attended a public meeting; 77 percent had voted in a national or state election; and 72 percent had participated in a protest or boycott.[8]

Also in the summer of 2003, I asked these young people if they would canvass again the following summer if they had the chance. More than 65 percent said that they were interested in canvassing in 2004. A year later, however, only about 14 percent of the 2003 summer canvassers were still working for the canvass, either full-time or as summer employees.

Of those canvassers who followed up with me in 2004, the median length of time that they had worked for the organization was about three months, or the length of a summer vacation from school. It is worth noting that this average is significantly higher than the national average for canvassers as a whole, which was reported by the canvassers themselves.[9] In the words of Doug, who was a field manager and trained new canvassers in the Ann Arbor office, "The national statistic is a canvasser lasts for two weeks." Although I was surprised by this statistic, a handful of canvassers cited this astonishingly high turnover rate during their interviews. One explanation for this statistical divergence is that I only had approval to study canvassers who had already completed their training and achieved staff status.[10] Canvassers and canvass directors around the country told me that only about 40 percent of the people who try out canvassing make it that far. Another explanation is that those who did not last very long as canvassers were less likely to respond to my request for a follow-up interview.[11]

Understanding the low retention rate of canvassers is simple: canvassing is very hard work, and many people are uncomfortable with the idea of raising money by standing on the street or going door to door. Even canvass directors who had worked for the organization for years recalled finding the job difficult when they started. Roy, a canvass director from the Portland office who had worked for the Project for over two years, remembered: "I came in, started, I hated it, I hated it."

The People's Project is constantly recruiting, and just about everyone who comes in for an interview is invited to try out the job. According to Lori, a director in the San Diego office: "We hire almost everyone, and I'd say . . . the only people that we really don't hire are folks that are considerably inappropriate." Even though almost everyone who applies is invited to try out the job as an observer, because the organization's advertisements do not fully describe the work, a large portion of the people who come in for an interview do not return. Lori, who had recently graduated from a liberal arts college in the Midwest, shared her observations about the retention rate in San Diego: "There's maybe a 50–60 percent chance that [interviewees] will actually come in for an observation day, [and a] 50 percent chance . . . that they will actually come in for their first day of work, so people really self-select."[12]

Even after choosing to try out canvassing, however, there is a very high attrition rate during the training period. Many people quit because they are not comfortable. Irina, a 20-year-old college student who was working for the San Diego canvass, reported: "Most people figure out whether they can do this or they can't on their second day, honestly, if not their first . . . Most folks quit after their second or third day." Others are let go because they don't meet the quota requirements. Lori pointed out that the Project's policies contribute to the high attrition rate during the training period: "If they don't make a certain amount of money within their first day or two, then we fire them." As a result of the quota requirement and people deciding that they do not want to canvass, Roy in Portland reported that only 60 percent of the trainees made it through the training process.

Once canvassers complete the training, however, many have a hard time with the job's long hours. As noted earlier, the average workday of a summer canvasser is much longer than eight hours. Canvassers begin their day at the office in the late morning. After arriving, they "warm up" by practicing the script and their delivery for about an hour. Next, they attend a staff meeting, which includes the daily announcements. After the staff meeting, canvassers disperse to their assigned neighborhoods, where they spend about an hour eating lunch together before beginning the canvassing. Five hours later they return to the office, record their day's work, and check out with a manager, who is responsible for confirming that the canvassers are fulfilling their monetary targets.

In addition to these mandatory eight hours, canvassers are expected to do campaign work earlier in the day and to participate in organized social events on most evenings after they have checked out. Counting these additional activities for which they receive no compensation, many canvassers reported working over sixty hours a week.

Beyond the long hours and the difficulty some people had raising quota, a number of canvassers found the pay excessively low. Kevin, from the Portland office, explained how the salary affects who stays at the job: "I mean everybody applies for the job, but the ones who stick with it . . . tend to be young, active, socially, environmentally, and . . . community-conscious people . . . who have few expenses because it doesn't pay a lot." There is no question that the nature of the work and the pay structure influence who chooses to canvass. In general, this type of work attracts a demographic of young people who do not have significant financial constraints.

Although I observed a diverse group of people—from different back-grounds, races, and ages—come through the door, those who achieved staff status during the summer 2003 canvass were not particularly diverse: 84 percent were white, and many said they lived with their parents while working for the People's Project.[13] While I was visiting the Atlanta canvass office, for example, two African American men and an African American woman came in to try out working in the predominantly white canvass office as observers. During the initial information session, I heard the woman ask if there were any noncanvassing positions available. The following day, none of them returned for the training. When I spoke with the only African American member of the 2003 cohort, Damon, who was working at the Ann Arbor canvass during the summer between his first and second years of college, he described how his race affected his canvassing:

> Canvassing as an African American male . . . I always felt that I had to be a little faster or . . . a little bit more than the average person if I wanted to succeed. I also have actually realized, and it was almost like a revelation, just how segregated we really are. [I've seen] folks that are afraid when you get to their door, just by looking at you . . . [They decide] that they're not going to answer the door . . . and also I think that maybe a lot of people . . . aren't even comfortable with giving money or giving a check to an African American male at their door.

Although those who stayed at the job tended to have fewer financial constraints, many canvassers found the low pay troubling. James, who had worked for the San Diego office in the summer of 2003 for about six weeks, estimated that "those who had [a mixture of] bad days and good days were making roughly minimum wage." He calculated that on bad days, when he was unable to sign up even one member, he was "making between three and four dollars an hour."

The low pay takes a toll on most canvassers. The only way Blanca was able to live on her salary, for example, was by sharing a room in a house with her sister: "We're sharing a room, splitting rent . . . I need to make sure that I'm making enough money . . . Right now, my rent is $200 a month and it's really manageable, even when you don't make that much here." Although Blanca was able to adjust her lifestyle to fit her limited pay, Caleb decided to leave the Atlanta office after canvassing for about a month and a half: "I was breaking even pretty much, and that was not acceptable."

Some canvassers also found that the work was too strenuous, noting the physical toll it took on their bodies. Mike, at 33 one of the oldest canvassers working in the Atlanta office, said: "I'm in pretty good shape but . . . I'm getting to a point where my knees hurt and my feet hurt." Mike was one of only three people in the sample of canvassers over 30, and he was the only full-timer (the other two were directors who did not canvass every day). A number of canvassers recalled "older people" not making it through the training process because they found the work too hard on their bodies. Those who were less physically fit also found the work challenging. Those who played on college sports teams during the school year seemed to find the work easier; some even found that canvassing helped them stay in shape during the summer months and prepared them for the beginning of the fall season.

Finally, some canvassers left after a short time or decided not to return the following summer because they were uneasy with the organization's politics and the way the offices were run. Figure 1 presents a model of canvasser attrition that includes estimations of attrition when they were provided by the canvassers.

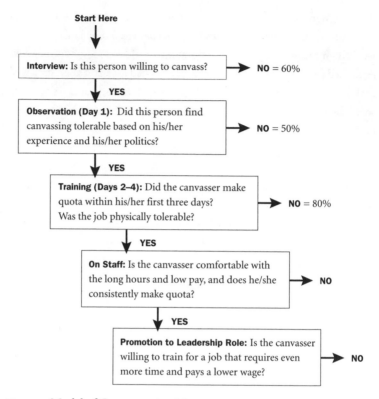

Figure 1. Model of Canvasser Attrition.

What Did They Do When They Left?

The young people who left the canvass went on to a variety of jobs: a few went abroad through school programs; others took school-related internships that were more in line with their career goals; some reported preparing to enter graduate school; and several found jobs that would allow them to make more money for less work. Many former canvassers reported working for restaurants or in retail. Diane, who planned to start college in the fall, left the Boulder canvass to work at Urban Outfitters on Pearl Street. She recalled telling customers that she had once been a street canvasser: "Later on, when I was working for Urban [Outfitters], I'd be like 'I was a canvasser' and they would kind of roll their eyes and be like 'oh . . . [the] annoying guys on the street who would bother us every day.'"

A small percentage found other work in politics after canvassing. Daniel, who had a master's degree, explained that he left the Ann Arbor canvass after a month to work on a political candidate's campaign. Another canvasser who stayed in politics after leaving the canvass was Tiffany, a 20-year-old high school graduate who worked in the Portland campaign office for about nine months. She explained her decision to quit canvassing saying, "I left because I was getting really burned out . . . I didn't feel like I needed to be sacrificing my health to be out there every single day talking to people . . . It was taking an emotional and psychic toll on me, as well as physical. So I decided that I kind of had had enough." Though she burned out on canvassing, Tiffany still wanted to work for progressive politics, but she spent the next four months unemployed before finding a job she liked. When I spoke with her in the summer of 2004, Tiffany was working for a local group "to get progressive initiatives on the ballot." One of the things she liked most about this job, which also involved going door to door, was the pay: "I'm just mostly excited that they actually pay their people something that they can afford to live on." And there were other advantages: "I work thirty-five hours a week . . . and I get to take an hour lunch on my own time while I'm out canvassing."

Others, however, believed their future political work options were constrained by a noncompetition agreement that the People's Project made them sign when they began working for the campaign office.[14] After signing this agreement, some canvassers thought that they were unable to work for other political groups. For example, when I followed up with Laurena from the Boulder canvass in 2004, she had made the transition from staff canvasser to director in the office. Even though she said that she "definitely would" consider working for one of the groups for whom she had fundraised, she told me: "[I] signed a contract that I can't do that for at least a year afterwards."

Mike, who had canvassed for the People's Project for over two years, had stronger feelings about the agreement, which he had to sign to receive his final paycheck from the organization:

They made me sign an extraordinarily corporate sort of noncompetition agreement . . . I had to sign this thing saying that I would promise not to canvass for anybody else for a year after I leave, and not to share any of the trade secrets of the [People's Project] and so forth and so on . . . [It] left a tremendously bad taste in my mouth. I ended up signing it because . . . I don't want to not get my last paycheck . . . and I'm on my way out, anyway, so why fight over it at this point? . . . [But the Project was] zealously guarding [its] corporate secrets as much as any Fortune 500 company.

Although during the summer of 2003 almost all the canvassers I spoke with felt they were making a difference, for many of them that feeling did not last. Brooks, a 19-year-old canvasser who had just finished his training in the Portland office when I spoke with him in 2003, was originally very enthusiastic about his work:

I'm out engaging, I'm out talking, I'm drawing awareness . . . [and] when I get home I'm sweaty and my bones ache a little bit and I look back at what I've done and I say: well, I could be putting my energy into making lattes, you know, at Starbucks . . . During high school, I worked at . . . a family law firm . . . and I came home . . . [and] I felt like . . . "What did that go into?" Now, I come back and, you know, it might even be my hardest day of work . . . but I feel like, "Yes, it's gone into *something*.

Brooks ended up canvassing for the entire summer of 2003. A year later, however, reflecting on his experience with the People's Project, he was much less enthusiastic about canvassing and working in politics more generally: "I left the experience knowing that that kind of grassroots activism isn't my cup of tea . . . It's not something I would partake in again . . . [I] became a little bit embittered by the businesslike approach . . . Your performance is totally evaluated on the money you bring in." When I spoke with him during the summer of 2004, Brooks was happily putting his energy into making lattes at Starbucks.

Although Brooks had found a job that made him happy, his leaving politics to pour coffee is distressing because his experience is not unique among canvassers. In fact, a number of the canvassers I met in summer 2003 had decided to work outside of politics by the time I spoke with them again in 2004.

As the People's Project has started running an increasing number of canvasses on behalf of national progressive groups, the experiences of its motivated and idealistic workforce have become more important. Indeed, the future of progressive politics in America is in the hands of a generation of young people who are being burned out and exploited by an employer whose ostensible goal is to strengthen the base of causes and campaigns that brought those same young people into the Project's offices.

Chapter 4

Outsourcing Activism
Politics and the Bottom Line

Throughout the eight years of the Clinton administration, funding for progressive causes waned. With a Democrat in the White House after twelve years of Republican rule, many Americans felt as if they no longer needed to support progressive causes.[1] In order to continue to exist, progressive groups needed to find a way to raise funds and maintain their membership base. The People's Project expanded to fill the void, providing a foolproof model for raising money and sustaining a grassroots base.

Although some national progressive groups, such as the Sierra Club and Greenpeace, had originally run their own independent campaign offices, they ended up closing down their own grassroots campaigns and hiring the People's Project during the 1990s. Jerry, a representative from the Project's national office, explained how the partnership works: "The groups that we run canvasses for, they pick their campaigns, we run their campaigns for them. We certainly give them our input as to what we think will be effective fundraisers and/or recruiters of staff . . . but it's their decision as to what campaigns they want to run, and our job is to run it." He acknowledged a recent trend to consolidate canvassing: "There [are] very few groups that have canvasses [left] . . . Fewer than . . . there used to be . . . ten or twenty years ago."

In each canvassing office, canvassers are told about the relationship between the People's Project and the groups on whose behalf they are fundraising during the training period. Kevin, a college graduate who had been working out of the Portland office as a canvasser for almost two years, told me how he presented this relationship to his trainees: "We obviously have nothing to hide, so I just explain very simply that we're a fundraising organization, and so it's more cost-effective and all-around beneficial for these groups to use us to raise money for them instead of hiring their own staff to go out and do it. People tend to understand pretty quickly once you explain that."

Kevin's account was corroborated during my meetings with representatives of the national progressive groups who hired the Project. Once hired, the People's Project applied its standardized model of grassroots campaigning, coordinating paid canvassers to be the foot soldiers for many groups in the progressive movement. The groups that outsource their campaigns to the Project no longer run local offices or train canvassers to conduct grassroots outreach. Instead, progressive groups looking to save money while raising it have only to sign up with the People's Project and trained canvassers will go door to door or stand on the street on their behalf, wearing T-shirts that display their logo or message.

Although they are one of the largest groups running outsourced canvasses, the People's Project is not the only one. At least two other unrelated groups are running such paid canvasses. Together these canvasses maintain a grassroots base for approximately 25 percent of the largest membership organizations in the United States.[2] Most of these groups are unions and professional associations, such as the American Federation of State, County, and Municipal Employees (AFSCME) and the Association of Trial Lawyers of America. They have a built-in membership base and do not need to rely on outsourced canvassing to sustain their numbers. But member-based organizations that do not have a built-in constituency must carry on nonstop membership drives. During the summer of 2003, in addition to running campaigns for numerous state groups, the People's Project ran campaigns for the national offices of Greenpeace USA, Save the Children, the Human Rights Campaign, and the Sierra Club.

Connecting Members to National Groups That Outsource

The main reason national progressive groups hire the People's Project is to increase their membership base. Even though each campaign is different, the standardized canvassing model yields canvassers who make quota, and the campaigns run by the People's Project are relatively successful. Some groups had never used canvassing as an outreach tactic before hiring the Project and deciding to outsource to develop a grassroots presence. Others, however, had already run grassroots campaigns themselves.

The first national group to outsource its canvass to the People's Project—the Sierra Club—fell into this second category. Jessica Hodge, a field representative for the group, explained the club's decision to close down its own canvass and outsource:

> We were doing it and we decided to subcontract because running a canvass is a lot of work and it was easier to have another group that was very good at it and wanted to do it, and had the same goals as we have . . . [Our canvass was originally] a moving canvass: you go into an area, you open an area, you open an office, you do the canvass, [and then] you close the office.

As one of the largest conservation groups in the United States, the Sierra Club maintains local chapters in every state and Puerto Rico. When the moving canvass was in areas where it had a local chapter, Hodge said it worked out of the Sierra Club's local office. However, even though the canvass sometimes shared a chapter's office, the "canvasses [were] run completely separate." The group's local chapters were "totally grassroots-run and the decisions come from the [local people]," this field representative explained, and the staff and volunteers of the local chapters were not involved in any way with the canvass.[3] Since the People's Project ran numerous local campaign offices around the country for the explicit purpose of canvassing, outsourcing to the Project was a logical move: during a period of time, canvassers in these offices around the country would spend their days raising funds and signing up members for the Sierra Club. In this way, the People's Project could keep more offices open year-round and the Sierra Club could maintain its grassroots base.

Greenpeace decided to close down its canvass for similar reasons. Mike, a canvasser in the Atlanta office who had worked for the Greenpeace canvass for four years in the early 1990s, explained: "Greenpeace was going door to door themselves . . . They had thirty offices around the country at one point, there were about twenty left when ours was shut down. At that point, it contracted to eight, and now they are no more. I was actually the canvass director of that office for . . . the last year and a half that it was open." The executive director of Greenpeace USA, John Passacantando, added to this explanation of why the group decided to close down its in-house canvass: "It was running at a huge loss . . . One of my predecessors had to make an absolutely horrible decision and shut down the legend-ary Greenpeace canvass, but the fact is that somebody was going to have to do it. You can't run something in the red forever, it goes down." Both men exalted the group's model of canvassing, which, in the words of Mike, had no "training process per se . . . there was no [Script]" and was what Passacantando called "this wild loosey-goosey canvass," but in the end it was not economically sustainable. After exploring other options for main-taining its grassroots outreach, Greenpeace decided to outsource to the People's Project in the early 2000s.

Unlike the Greenpeace and Sierra Club canvassing models, campaigns run by the People's Project were successful at raising money. In fact, rep-resentatives from all of the national groups that had outsourced to the Project were pleased with the ways that it expanded their bases. John Pas-sacantando spoke about its success: "[The People's Project] helped us build our new financial base . . . It gave us a new base and it paid approximately 25 percent of our yearly income from monthly electronic donations, which is huge." Similarly, Sally Green Heaven of the Human Rights Campaign spoke about the success of the canvassing efforts the Project had run on its behalf since the late 1990s: "I started here in '99. I think we had about 200,000 [members] . . . and then it's just grown so explosively every year that I've been here and, you know, it's been because we've been partner-ing with the [People's Project]." By May 2005, the HRC's membership had grown to include over 600,000 people, about half of whom had been recruited through the canvass.[4]

Although the People's Project had successfully raised funds and increased membership for these national groups, it is unclear how much local engagement came from such outsourced campaigns. All of the groups provided their members with information, usually in the form of a periodic magazine. In addition, most told me that they contacted their new members directly about becoming more active participants in their campaigns. Although they inquired about further engagement, the groups' leaders recognized that a significant proportion of their members only wanted to contribute money. These observations are consistent with the findings of scholars such as Robert Putnam, who concluded that the "explosive growth in interest groups represented in Washington . . . is not really a counterexample to the supposed decline in social connectedness," because "these are not really associations in which members meet one another."[5] In fact, many Americans who contribute to these so-called tertiary organizations are not interested in participating at all.

Speaking about his experience as the president of the HRC, for example, Joe Solmonese said that he could classify members of his group into two types, those who only wanted to give money and those who wanted to give more:

> You could . . . divide it between two different kinds of people . . . someone who [will say] . . . "I'm a member, [I] will send my money in, and I don't ever want to do one thing," or someone who says, "I'm going to sign up at a [Lesbian, Gay, Bisexual, and Transgender] Pride [Event] . . . and give my e-mail address. I'm going to get involved. I want to do things. I want to get the action alerts, I want to e-mail my congressman, and I want to go stand on a streetcorner and hold signs."

Similarly, John Passacantando of Greenpeace observed that many of his group's members did not want to get involved: "Some people just say . . . I don't want to come out on an action, I don't want to be out in the forest, I'm funding you to do this . . . We give [our members] the chance, we make the offer. But we have found that there are people who want to be activists and there are people who just want to give money."

For some national groups, contributions of money are enough. The mission of Save the Children, for example, is to create "real and lasting change for children in need."[6] As such, the fundamental goal of this group's outsourced canvass is to fund programs for disadvantaged children. All the group asks of those recruited by canvassers is a monthly contribution. Most of the other national groups outsourcing their canvasses in 2003, however, aim to do more than raise money; they also have political goals.

As Jerry from the Project's national office described, in addition to helping these national progressive groups raise money, the canvass will also "help them win their campaigns" through advocacy and lobbying. Thus the goals of their grassroots campaigns are to raise funds *and* gain political clout by adding members on whose behalf the groups' lobbyists can speak.[7]

In other words, most of these groups have explicitly political goals. Some of their political campaigns are centrally run by the groups' national offices. Others, like those run by the Sierra Club and the Human Rights Campaign, are coordinated through decentralized local chapters and local steering committees that had "organically developed" over the years (Sally Green Heaven, May 2005). These political campaigns ran the gamut of progressive issues and geographic scales, including national campaigns about global warming, state-focused campaigns on marriage-related bills, local election campaigns, and ballot initiatives. Although one underlying reason for running a canvass is to gain political support for a campaign in a local area, state, or congressional district, it is unclear how members who have been recruited via the outsourced canvass actually get involved. Even though representatives of these national groups told me that many of their members had signed up to receive e-mail about the groups' campaigns and their particular political actions, they were unable to say what percentage of their members actually *participated* beyond giving money.

In fact, as one of the top political consultants who worked on John Kerry's presidential campaign pointed out, when he asked these national groups to mobilize their members to participate in the presidential campaign's local events, he was disappointed by the outcome: "*None* of these organizations can actually produce two bodies . . . when they need to." This finding has been corroborated by the work of scholars such as Margaret Weir and Marshall Ganz, who write that these large membership-based groups "have had difficulty mobilizing [their members] to take effective political action."[8] Given their failure to elicit action from their members, it is unclear how much actual political clout should be assigned to these national groups based on their membership numbers. If these progressive groups cannot even get their members to participate in a local event for the Democratic candidate for president, it is unclear how many of them can be counted on to do much more than sign an electronic petition. Therefore, threats by these national groups' lobbyists that their members will strike, protest, or even vote according to their position on an issue could be called into question.

The disconnect between the national groups and their members is nothing new. Scholarly research on the ways Americans engage civically points out that the connection between local members and national groups has atrophied.[9] Instead of relying on their members to get their work done, national groups today rely on paid staff, who are funded by the money that comes in via direct mail, telemarketing, and canvassing. By outsourcing their outreach tactics, these groups have significantly increased the distance between progressive Americans and politics today. In other words, most members recruited through canvassing do not develop personal ties to the organizations they join. True membership involves more than making a monetary contribution; it includes meaningful engagement and action at the local, regional, and/or national levels.

The gulf between national groups and their members did not begin with the outsourcing of canvassing. Even when these organizations ran their own canvasses, their members were not necessarily any more engaged. While the Sierra Club was running its own canvass, for example, it kept the work of its local chapters, which are run predominantly by volunteers, strictly separate from its fundraising efforts. This division ensured that Sierra Club members were much less connected to the actual work of the national group than they could have been.[10] Although some members who were recruited via the moving canvass likely became involved in the work of their local chapters, because the chapters were disconnected from the fundraising, the links between members and chapters were not built into the process.

This separation between local action and fundraising has become an issue for Greenpeace USA. When I met with him in May 2005, John Passacantando discussed the implications of his group's decision to outsource its canvass and hire the People's Project to run its grassroots campaigns. In his opinion, Greenpeace had essentially disconnected its grassroots fundraising from its grassroots activism: "I think it's dangerous to separate your fundraising. If you separate your fundraising too much, you can lose your integrity, right? Your fundraising has to be built around what you really care about, what you really want to do." Although he recognized the dangers of outsourcing, this director of one of the more progressive environmental groups in the United States also understood that fundraising is a necessary component of running political campaigns in the twenty-first century:[11] "Our challenge is how can we be as sophisticated globally as Ford Motor Company, . . . General Electric, or Exxon Mobil . . . But, we still have to have that spirit [of challenging them]. If we lose that spirit, then we're just selling calendars, right? And so that's a day-to-day challenge [of raising funds and maintaining integrity]." In part, as a result of the need to keep Greenpeace's fundraising and activism connected, along with the fact that the members who had signed up through the outsourced canvass "weren't staying on long enough," the group decided to end its contract with the People's Project. As of December 2004, Greenpeace was no longer running an outsourced canvass.[12] Although Passacantando called Greenpeace's choice to conclude its contract with the Project "an economic decision," he also acknowledged a major unintended consequence of the outsourcing of grassroots campaigns: national groups that severed the connection between their fundraising and activism made engagement more difficult and increased the distance between themselves and their members.

The problem is exacerbated by the Project's reliance on "geoflexible" canvass directors who are regularly moved from one office to another. Instead of relying on locals who are familiar with the extant networks of progressive groups in their home areas and might even have personal connections with them, the canvass counts on rootless workaholics who are centrally managed by the Project's national and regional offices. By moving its canvass directors around and not investing in true connections to local communities, it is not surprising that the People's Project is unable to engage locally recruited members in meaningful ways.

Running an Outsourced Canvass

The standardized canvassing model of the People's Project assumes that "anybody who can walk, talk, and carry a clipboard" can become an effective activist (Mike, 33, Atlanta canvass). It makes it possible for the organization to get canvassers trained quickly and out on the streets raising money and support for their grassroots campaigns within hours. Although most posters and flyers for the People's Project advertise jobs for the environment, with the consolidation of canvassing the campaigns that are being run out of the Project's local offices do not necessarily focus on environmental protection. Each campaign is different, and the organization runs canvasses of varying lengths. The canvassers I spoke to in the summer of 2003 had worked on issues as diverse as child welfare, same-sex marriage initiatives, urban sprawl, drinking water protection, international toxic-chemical usage, and deforestation. A director in the Portland office, Will, who had started working for the organization as a canvasser in 2000, recalled that, since joining the organization: "I've probably worked on twenty or thirty different issues in two and a half years." Not only did Will work on many campaigns but, during his time in the Portland office, he had also canvassed on behalf of numerous groups.[13]

Smaller canvass offices, such as the 2003 Baltimore and Ann Arbor offices, run only one campaign at a time.[14] As a result, the young people who respond to the organization's standardized job flyers, which are posted around town during the summer and on college campuses when the organization is recruiting in the spring, end up working on whatever campaign the national and regional offices have decided to run out of that canvassing office when they start. Eileen, who had just finished her junior year of college and worked for the Ann Arbor office of the People's Project, for example, was not particularly inspired by the campaign under way when she worked there. Originally attracted by the idea of working for the environment, she had hoped to work on issues related to clean air. Instead, Eileen ended up working to protect open spaces from development for three weeks until she was let go for not making quota. "Quite honestly," she said, "I'm only doing this, or working on this issue, because that's what the office is working on. I think there are really other . . . more important issues." For Eileen, those issues were environmental, but canvassers in smaller offices are expected to work on whatever is the campaign of the day; they have no choice.

In contrast, larger offices run multiple campaigns for different national groups simultaneously. In the large Portland office of the People's Project, they were "working on anywhere from, like, three to five different issues at any one time" (Will, 30, Portland canvass). When an office runs more than one campaign concurrently, as is common during the summer, the directors assign a canvasser to a campaign based on the needs of the office and/or the canvasser's interests. As a result, some young people who were attracted by the idea of making money while trying to help the environment found themselves working on unrelated campaigns.

Paul had just finished his sophomore year at an elite West Coast school and was recruited during the school year to work for the People's Project. He recalled being very interested in the particular environmental campaign that the recruiters visiting his school said would be the focus of the summer's campaign: "It looked like a very, very good summer job . . . They were concentrating especially on Arctic drilling and, considering how much of the forest has been destroyed in my country and the exploitation of my country, it really bothered me that they would be [cutting down forests to drill for oil] here in the United States." Paul's personal experience growing up in Honduras had inspired him to work on environmental protection, but when he arrived at the office he was assigned to work on child welfare issues instead: "I ended up working for Save the Children as opposed to environmental issues." Despite this change, Paul was happy with his job: "The environment is important to me, but at the same time, Save the Children was a lot closer to home and . . . you don't get a lot of the mean responses [like] you do if you come up to maybe a logger's house . . . [when you're canvassing for] the Sierra Club . . . Most of the people are supportive, which is nice."

Other canvassers, however, did not find such a good fit. Some even recalled being asked to work on campaigns that they did not support. Tiffany in the Portland office remembered being moved from one campaign to another:

> They would just take you off of a campaign you were working on and stick you on another one, and you didn't really have discretion over that. If you're going into a job . . . because you truly believe in it, you want to

be doing something that's true to your ethics and OK for you. I wasn't necessarily totally comfortable working for the Sierra Club. I'm not a huge fan of theirs . . . I expressed discomfort about doing it and they were just, like, "Well, we need you to."

Being moved from one canvass to another was not unique to Tiffany's experience. Representatives from the national groups that were outsourcing to the People's Project were well aware that the canvassers were working on multiple campaigns for different groups simultaneously. In the words of Joe Solmonese, the president of the Human Rights Campaign, for example: "The person who is out standing on the streetcorner trying to sign you up to join HRC . . . they honestly, like the next day, might be doing the same thing for [a different organization]." After working for about seven months out of the Portland office of the People's Project, Jason, a 24-year-old college graduate, agreed: "In a given week, I'll canvass on three different campaigns."

For canvassers like Tiffany and Jason who were bounced from one campaign to another, sometimes without warning, keeping track of the specifics of the grassroots campaigns they were working on could be very difficult. Representatives of the national groups that hired the People's Project to run their campaigns worked with the organization to maintain a consistent message by providing information as well as running briefings for the local offices from time to time. How effective such training was, however, was unknown. During my meetings with representatives of the outsourcing groups, a number of them wondered how much information actually trickled down to the young people who were going door to door or standing on the streets.

Speaking about the ways that the HRC provides information to the canvassers who are fundraising on its behalf, for example, Sally Green Heaven, the deputy field director of the group, considered the limitations: "In practice, I guess I wonder how much it penetrated, like to the level of the canvasser that was out in every city . . . The kind of training that we provided was mostly phone briefings." This national field director also recalled the group running in-person training sessions from time to time, but since the lifespan of the average canvasser is only a few weeks, it is unlikely that many canvassers benefited from such briefings. In fact, most of the young people who were canvassing on behalf of the HRC on any given day probably had neither received a phone briefing nor participated in any in-person training. Other outsourcing groups faced similar challenges. According to Jessica Hodge, the Washington, D.C., field representative for the Sierra Club: "The only real connection is [between] the canvass director in the local office [of the People's Project] and the Sierra Club office."

Perhaps in part to address the suspected limitations of the diffusion of information, the People's Project tries to maintain consistency across campaigns. As such, all campaigns rely on Scripts that are almost identical. Because the Scripts are easy to learn, canvassers can be easily moved from campaign to campaign. Besides learning a different Script for each campaign, however, canvassers reported not receiving much additional training about the group or the campaign before being shuffled from one campaign to another.

Hailey, an 18-year-old canvasser who was working out of the Portland office, for example, had spent her first two weeks canvassing for a clean water campaign in the office. She spoke about being switched without undergoing any training: "They just sent me out there . . . I learned the [Script] and they sent me out there." Her concerns were particularly warranted as canvassers reported that each campaign had a different quota—some significantly higher than others. Although Hailey told me she was worried about meeting the quota of the new campaign, she reported: "I did well that day, so I was OK with it, I was like 'whatever.'" Without learning much about the organization or the campaign for which she was to raise funds, Hailey was able to meet the requirements of the new campaign by using her canvassing skills and the campaign's Script alone.

Even directors who had been working out of the Portland office for much longer than Hailey had limited knowledge of some of the organizations and campaigns the office was running in the summer of 2003. On the day that I interviewed him, Roy was planning to canvass on behalf of Save the Children. A representative of Save the Children had told me that, in order to maintain the integrity of her group's "brand," the group visited canvassing offices "as needed throughout the year." However, these visits did not seem particularly effective in providing information to those who were doing the actual fundraising—not even to a long-term member of the canvass like Roy. When I asked him about the group for whom he would be fundraising that evening, he replied: "Yeah I don't know too much . . . You probably know as much as I do." Although his lack of information did not give me much confidence in the national group's "training visits," Roy did not seem too concerned about his lack of knowledge. In fact, he was confident in his ability to recruit support for Save the Children: "I read all [of the group's] literature, I can express to people at the door, and I got the [Script] to say. [I'll] smile [and they'll] write checks."

At least for Hailey and Roy, the lack of training did not seem to interfere with their ability to canvass well and recruit members. Beyond fundraising, however, it is unclear how effective canvassers can be in building grassroots support for these campaigns when they have such limited knowledge of and passion for them. Given the canvassers' inadequate understanding of the national groups and their political campaigns, it is likely that the outsourcing of canvassing has widened rather than narrowed the disconnect between these national groups and their members.

Narrowing the Local Channels into National Politics

The consolidation of canvassing has also affected the channels through which interested young people can enter progressive politics. As I learned from my former student Laura's experience, competition for even an entry-level position in a national progressive group's Washington, D.C., office is fierce. Every year, college graduates converge on the nation's capital to find jobs working in progressive politics. Many go looking for work at the national or legislative headquarters of a progressive group whose issues interest them. Unfortunately, paying jobs are limited, and, for those applicants without some personal connection to a national group, the majority of entry-level positions in these Washington offices are unpaid internships.[15] In the words of Jessica Hodge of the Sierra Club, many young people come to Washington "because they want to work on national policy . . . We definitely have a lot of people that used to be interns here now . . . [Our office has] a ton of them actually." Of the forty paid staff members in the group's legislative office in Washington, D.C., she estimated that one-quarter of them began their work there as interns.[16]

There are, however, a limited number of paid jobs for recent college graduates in national progressive politics. The People's Project partners with groups that run a handful of paid programs for recent graduates to gain experience in grassroots organizing at the local, state, and national levels. These jobs have become increasingly competitive in recent years. They include a fellowship program and the campus organizer program, both of which require three months of canvass directing during the summer.[17] In addition, the organization partners with the Green Corps program, which calls itself the "field school for environmental organizing."[18] Through Green Corps, college graduates are placed in paid positions in environmental groups for nine months of the year. As with the People's Project's other partnerships, Green Corps members are expected to serve as canvass directors, running local campaign offices during the summer months. In all of the canvass offices I visited around the country in the summer of 2003, approximately half of the canvass directors were working on the canvass through one of these three programs.

Jessica Hodge of the Sierra Club said her group worked closely with young people enrolled in this program: "[Green Corps is] really intensive. [Its organizers are] kind of poverty-stricken, [working] like sixty and seventy hours a week." Although the work is hard, the year-long program is successful in placing those who complete it in national groups. Hodge reported that "lots and lots" of the graduates of this program had gone on to work for the Sierra Club.

An alumna of the program who was working for a progressive environmental group in Washington, D.C., explained to me Green Corps' attraction to recent college graduates: It "actively recruits talent and then effectively works to launch long-term careers in grassroots organizing and advocacy. It's also an effective avenue for networking between liberal environmental groups because alumni have a fairly well developed sense of loyalty to one another, and confidence that fellow alumni are talented and well trained."[19] Even this full-time employee of a progressive group in Washington admitted to having "mixed feelings" about her experience with Green Corps. But she acknowledged: "[I] would not be working for [this group] right now if I hadn't done Green Corps."

Others had less positive experiences with the program. In the winter 2004 edition of *Threshold*, the magazine of the Student Environmental Action Coalition, Nathaniel Miller, a former Green Corps organizer, cautioned students against applying to the group. He wrote that during the four months that he worked with Green Corps "they engaged in union-busting and openly opposed affirmative action, environmental justice, and other efforts to diversify the environmental movement." In fact, many of this recent college graduate's complaints about Green Corps were reminiscent of those I heard from the People's Project canvassers in 2003. He called Green Corps a "top-down organization" that required its workers to meet quantitative goals and targets, and he accused the group of having a "fundamentally undemocratic" structure. Although when hired he had been ecstatic to find a position where he would "get paid to be an activist," he was let go after reportedly trying to organize the members of his cohort and being a union agitator.[20]

Although Miller's short tenure suggests that his personal experience with the group may be unique, I found similar accounts posted on the progressive watchdog website Nonprofit Watch.[21] This site posts personal reports and maintains a bulletin board of accounts by other young people. In contrast to claims by some on the left that this website is a front for some right-wing organization, it is not. It is run by Bernardo Issel, a self-proclaimed progressive who works for the labor-union-organizing group Corporate Campaign, Inc.[22] In his article, Miller also reported that Green Corps had a very high attrition rate. In his class of thirty-one people, "only fourteen finished the year, [with] six people leaving during the first three weeks."[23] In short, young people working for this partner group, which states its mission as training "the next generation of environmental leaders,"[24] have had problems similar to those of People's Project employees. Some who did not complete the year-long program had been so turned off by their experience with Green Corps that they were no longer interested in working for mainstream progressive politics and became anarchists instead.[25]

It is much easier to get an entry-level job at the local level than paid work in a national office. Jessica Hodge of the Sierra Club, for example, began as an unpaid volunteer in the Las Vegas chapter. She recalled slowly making her way into a leadership position at the local level and then, after four years, moving to Washington to take a paid position in the group's legislative office as a field representative.

Hodge's experience mirrors the observations of Theda Skocpol and her colleagues in their work on the institutional origins of civic engagement in the United States: "Local chapters [have historically] channeled indispensable resources of money and human energy to the 'higher' levels of federations."[26] Although Hodge was able to rise through local channels into national politics, she recognized that her personal experience had become less common in recent years: "I think I'm becoming more and more an exception . . . I wouldn't be surprised if I was one of the few [people in this office that started out as a Sierra Club volunteer in a local chapter]." In other words, her experience of entering into a national group by working her way through its local channels is unlike that of most people who have ended up working in the national offices of progressive groups in recent years.

For young people looking to start in a *paid* job in progressive politics at the local level, there are fewer options. In fact, canvassing for the People's Project provides one of the very few paid channels into left-leaning national groups from the local level. Before many national groups outsourced their canvasses, their local offices provided entry points for young people to get involved in progressive politics. John Passacantando of Greenpeace, for example, spoke to me about the ways that the in-house Greenpeace canvass had been important to his group and the role that it played in recruiting young people:

> The [Greenpeace] canvass served as a feeder track for hungry, smart people who would one day run Greenpeace campaigns [and even] run Greenpeace . . . We lost something huge when we shut down our canvass. It's not [a] secret. So many of the heavyweights throughout the Greenpeace world, Greenpeace U.S. and Greenpeace International Amsterdam, had

started in [our] canvass . . . [It] served an amazing purpose. [And we] are now tasked with [finding other ways] to bring people in.

The executive director listed a number of high-ranking staff at Greenpeace *and* other national environmental groups who had begun working in progressive politics as members of the Greenpeace canvass. Although the group had developed some newer programs to bring in young people, he recognized that they did not replace the canvass: "The volume that we had going on that canvass . . . [which] had brought in smart, young people who were hitting the doors every night, and who were ready to do action on a moment's notice, [such as] climbing action, ship action . . . We've not replaced that, and that remains a weakness [for us]."

With groups like Greenpeace outsourcing their canvasses, there are fewer and fewer options for young people to enter the local branches of national groups. At this point, young people who want to enter progressive politics at the local level through the canvass must succeed within the hierarchy of the People's Project to be promoted. The Project acknowledges this fact and even sees itself as a training ground for progressive activists. Jerry, from the group's national office, explained that the canvass is all about "training activists and . . . [it's] filling a void left by higher education in a lot of ways . . . Too many schools, I think, don't teach students basic citizenship skills . . . and/or having their voices heard, and/or working with their neighbors to get the decision implemented that they want . . . I see that as a . . . societal void that's filled by the [People's Project]." Even canvass directors in the local campaign offices of the organization saw the training of young people to be activists as one of their main jobs.

If they are successful within the Project, there are many opportunities for these young people to move up through the organization and its partners at the local, regional, and national levels. Jerry explained the role the canvass plays for his organization: "Most of our staff, period, whether they're senior, whether they're advocates, whether they're . . . in the whole [Project's] world, the vast majority of them have either canvassed or [been a] canvass director . . . The canvass is the backbone of all these groups." Idealistic young people who are willing to work long hours for limited pay and be moved around to fill the immediate needs of the People's Project are rewarded with positions within the progressive movement. For those young people who do not fit the canvassing organization's mold, however, there are very few other options.

When speaking with canvassers from the cohort of 2003, I asked whether, in the future, they would be willing to work for one of the national groups on whose behalf they had canvassed. Most enthusiastically responded that they would *definitely* work at an outsourcing group if they were given the chance. Some, though, were concerned that they were not legally permitted to take such a job.[27]

Although the canvassers were excited about working for the outsourcing groups, very few representatives of those national groups could name staff people in their offices who had started out as canvassers for the People's Project. A representative of Save the Children reported that such opportunities were unlikely because her group had no actual contact with the canvassers. Similarly, although John Passacantando said that Greenpeace was open to hiring people who had worked for their outsourced canvass, he noted that the canvass did not provide direct channels into his group because it was "such a separate entity." Other than those who had entered the Sierra Club through the Green Corps program, Jessica Hodge also could not recall any former canvassers from the People's Project working for her group at the local, regional, or national level.

The Human Rights Campaign provided the one exception. When asked about the possibility for members of their outsourced canvass coming to work for the national group, Sally Green Heaven replied: "Yeah, it has definitely happened. There are some canvassers who just really like the organization, and the work, and the message. [They] have applied for jobs and we've hired them. One of our former field organizers actually . . . had been a canvasser . . . so she canvassed for HRC and then she came here." Unfortunately, this example was the only account of a canvasser making the transition to working for an outsourcing group. This one example highlights just how narrow the channels of entry are for young people hoping to get into national progressive politics by working at the grassroots level. As such, it is not clear that the People's Project is doing such a great job of training the future leaders of the progressive movement.

Because so few national groups now run local offices that provide paid opportunities for idealistic young people, the People's Project has become the gatekeeper for many entry-level positions within national progressive groups. But many, perhaps too many, young people are being chewed up and spit out by this standardized model of activism that treats idealistic young people as interchangeable cogs in the machine of grassroots politics in America. The fact that it quickly burns out and turns off so many of its recruits adds to its negative effect on progressive politics.

In short, the outsourcing of canvassing has significantly limited the diversity of entry points into progressive politics from the grassroots level and, as more and more national groups outsource to the People's Project and a handful of organizations like it, the problem will only worsen. One case in point is provided by the Democratic National Committee (DNC). Before the 2004 presidential election, the People's Project spun off a for-profit group called Grassroots Campaigns, whose purpose was to raise funds and organize political campaigns by running canvasses.[28] The DNC was the organization's first client. When I met with Josh Wachs, who worked at the DNC as the executive director during the 2004 election and had been working with the Democratic Party for years, he told me about the decision to hire this organization and called the outsourced canvass a "prospecting program for donors."

This outsourcing of grassroots politics by the Democratic Party is the most recent step in the consolidation of activism that has become the norm for progressive politics in the United States. When a group's future leaders are treated like cogs, and their employers hire them out to "prospect" for donors, is it any wonder that the Left is fractured, disengaged, and losing the very fights they are raising money to win?

Chapter 5
Laying Sod versus Cultivating the Grass
A Postmortem on the 2004 Election

I f all politics truly *are* local, as the late speaker of the House Tip O'Neill once said, then the outsourcing of grassroots campaigns to the People's Project is the outsourcing of politics. By relying on managers who are not rooted in the areas in which they work and quickly burning through the young people who are canvassing for its campaigns, the outsourcing of politics is *not* good for politics. During the 2004 presidential race, the 3Ms were played out in full and, once again, the *members* mattered the most. In other words, more than the *message* or the *men* who ran for the office, the importance of the members and the ways the Republicans and the Democrats engaged them reaffirms the relevance of O'Neill's famous observation. One of the most popular explanations for the continued failure of progressive politics on the national stage and for the specific loss in the 2004 presidential campaign is that the Left lost its base at the local, grassroots level. I contend that it is the *way* that the members were contacted and mobilized that explains the disappointing outcome of recent elections for the Left.

While much of the grassroots outreach and mobilization on the left was outsourced to groups that hired paid canvassers, the Right mobilized what they purported to be an army of local volunteers to raise funds, run phone banks, and canvass for President George W. Bush. Although both the Left and the Right ran nationally centralized campaigns that included extensive canvassing efforts, for all intents and purposes those on the right were more effective: their candidate won the presidency and they increased the Republican majority in both houses of Congress. In particular, the Republican Party rallied the president's natural allies: social conservatives whose votes were determined by their religious and moral beliefs and economic conservatives whose choices were driven by fiscal policies. To ensure success, the party mobilized its allies using a densely connected network of local volunteers through what the Republican Party called the "72-hour plan" to mobilize the grassroots constituency of the party. Bush's political adviser Karl Rove is said to have called the plan "the most ambitious grassroots model in the party's history."[1] This plan, known to many as the "Amway model of multilevel marketing of the President," involved recruiting Bush supporters—both young and old—through a complex network of local volunteers.[2]

In contrast to the Republicans' cultivation of preexisting grassroots networks, the Democrats took shortcuts, laying sod at the local level to make up for their lack of political infrastructure and true grassroots. As is becoming increasingly apparent, laying sod in the form of outsourced political workers and imported volunteers cannot compete with true grassroots connections among like-minded neighbors.

Campaign Strategies and Political Infrastructure in 2004

One significant difference between the 2004 election and those that preceded it was the appearance of "527 groups," which played an important role in both the Republican and Democratic strategies. Although these private, tax-exempt political groups have been around since Section 527 was added to the Internal Revenue Code in 1974, they only became crucial to political campaigns after the Bipartisan Campaign Reform Act of 2002. This act, which is more commonly known as the McCain-Feingold Campaign Finance Reform law, was designed to address financial abuses that were common in political campaigns, along with the perception that money had become excessively influential in politics.[3] Once the legal challenges to McCain-Feingold by the National Rifle Association, among others, were resolved in May 2003, it prohibited the raising or spending of "soft money" by national party committees.[4] Because one of the main effects of the law was to ban corporate and private contributions, Section 527 was invoked by supporters of the Democratic and Republican candidates to establish political groups that *could* receive the financial backing of private donors. The purpose of these groups was to influence the elections outside of the political parties and, in many instances, political consulting firms were hired to achieve these goals.[5]

Although 527 groups in both parties raised and spent tens of millions of dollars, the strategies employed by the political groups on the left and the right were very different.[6] The 527 group that may have received the most attention during the election was the Swift Boat Veterans for Truth, which spent almost $23 million in 2004 on a media campaign "to counter the false 'war crimes' charges John Kerry repeatedly made against Vietnam veterans who served in our units and elsewhere, and to accurately portray Kerry's brief tour in Vietnam as a junior grade Lieutenant."[7] Along with the pro-Bush Progress for America Voter Fund, right-leaning groups flooded the media markets of swing states with anti-Kerry advertisements. According to a report published by the Washington, D.C.-based Center for Public Integrity in November 2004, "Section 527 organizations supporting President Bush spent nearly $30 million on broadcast ads in the final three weeks of the election . . . triple the amount spent by similar groups supporting Sen. John Kerry."[8]

In contrast to those right-leaning 527s that subsidized the media blitz in swing states, the 527 political groups on the left spent a significant portion of their money on grassroots outreach. The largest of these groups was the coalition of Democratic allies called America Coming Together (ACT), which ran what the *New York Times* called "the largest independently financed turnout drive in history."[9] Tom Lindenfeld, a political operative who held high-ranking positions in the Democratic Party during earlier elections and was one of the architects of ACT, explained how ACT and its sister group, America Votes, worked: "We took all the resources of all of our associate or allied [progressive] organizations and tried to create a sense of a traffic cop, so that we were making sure that all of the work that we were doing wasn't duplicative and that we were using it as effectively as possible . . . Then we could maximize collectively our impact, and that's what we did."

The overall mission of this 527 group is stated on its website as "building core political infrastructure [that] culminated in an army of over 100,000 staff and volunteers working on Election Day [2004] with common plans and voter targets."[10] In other words, instead of spending the majority of their money on media advertisements in swing states, this 527 group concentrated on increasing Democratic voter turnout and providing the infrastructure to mobilize voters from *outside* the Democratic Party. In this case, infrastructure came in the form of political organizers and paid canvassers who conducted voter registration and voter contact to get out the Democratic vote in swing states.

The issue of political infrastructure, however, extends well beyond the roles that the 527 groups played in the 2004 election. Political infrastructure involves all of the resources that make political campaigns work: financial, human, technological, and physical. Such an infrastructure begins with the voting base that is the grassroots membership of a constituency, connecting them to the political party at the state and national levels, as well as to the candidate. In their campaigns, the Democrats and Republicans started with and operated very different systems. As Lindenfeld suggests, much of the infrastructure on the left was generated by 527 groups, like ACT, rather than by the support system of the Democratic Party itself. The political infrastructure on the right, in contrast, was maintained by the Republican Party, with the assistance of some of its closest allies.

Since November 2004, the Left's weak political infrastructure has become a major topic of discussion among those considering how to rejuvenate the Democratic Party. Bill Bradley, the former Democratic senator from New Jersey, for example, called the Democrats "a party inverted." Focusing his comments on the importance of political infrastructure, the former senator describes it as "a stable pyramid [that extends] from the base up." He compares the "comprehensive structure" of the Republican Party with the weak infrastructure of the Democrats, reporting that Democratic candidates have "no coherent, larger structure that they can rely on." Bradley also implies that there are significant limitations to developing political infrastructure outside the Democratic Party, as was done during the 2004 elections, and he recognizes that building such a political infrastructure requires considerable financial resources. It is not, however, the money in and of itself that matters: "The money makes a difference because it goes toward reinforcing a structure that is already stable."[11] For the Democrats to win elections in the future, Bradley emphasizes that they will need to develop a lasting political infrastructure that is as well dispersed as that of the Right. Such an infrastructure, the former senator stresses, must include funding for research institutes, political strategists who coordinate the message and the platform of the party, and lasting roots that extend down to the level of the local voter.

The weakness of the political infrastructure on the left during the 2004 elections was widely recognized by the people I interviewed; both Democratic Party officials and those who were working outside the party emphasized the need to develop an effective political infrastructure that endures. Josh Wachs, who was executive director of the Democratic National Committee (DNC) during the 2004 election and had been working with the Democratic Party for years, linked this lack of political infrastructure to the eight years that Clinton was president. Reflecting on the status of the party after the Clinton presidency, he explained: "In 2001, [Terry] McAuliffe became DNC chair. We did an assessment and found that we didn't have infrastructure, so we had to build a financial infrastructure, a technological infrastructure, and a physical infrastructure." He explained that, in contrast, the Republicans had "been investing in infrastructure for years." Thus the Democratic Party's priority was to develop both the financial and the technological resources that would allow coordination at the national level.

Like this high-ranking party official, political consultant Laurie Moskowitz also emphasized the weakness of the political infrastructure on the left. Having directed the DNC's field effort for the Gore campaign in 2000 and having worked on the grassroots mobilization of progressive Americans during the 2004 campaign, she noted that there was very little time after the Democratic National Convention in July 2004 to lay the foundation for an infrastructure: "We were building from scratch . . . We need an organization that is looking at the bigger picture for how we organize on issues, and then [we must] build infrastructure around that." With experience mobilizing progressive voters from both inside and outside the Democratic Party, Moskowitz stressed the need for the Left to establish an infrastructure that endures beyond the election and links the national campaign directly to the states.

Even the leaders of progressive groups not directly working on the election recognized the need for the Democrats to develop a better infrastructure. The executive director of Greenpeace USA, John Passacantando stressed this point when we discussed the fallout from the 2004 elections. He likened political infrastructure to the complex system of arteries and veins that circulate blood to and from the heart: "The heart without the machinery, you can't get there."

In contrast to this generally recognized lack of infrastructure on the left, the Republicans have been cultivating the national party's infrastructure for years. It involves fundraising and paid professional mobilization capabilities that complement a dense network of local volunteers at the grassroots level around the country. These roots were originally cultivated, to some degree, in the early 1990s when Newt Gingrich collaborated with social conservative groups to develop and implement the Contract with America.[12] In many ways, this network integrated the extensive grassroots reach of the Christian Coalition. When *Time* magazine ran a profile of the Christian Coalition's executive director, Ralph Reed, in 1993, it quoted Reed as saying: "Our ambition is to be larger and more effective than both political parties combined."[13] Although it is unclear if it actually achieved such a lofty goal, there is no question that the interests of Christian conservatives have become more central to the Republican Party in recent years. In 2001, in fact, Reed was elected chairman of the Georgia Republican Party.[14] In December 2003 the *Atlanta Journal-Constitution* published an article about Reed, who had begun chairing the Bush campaign for the Southeast region. The newspaper reported that Reed was brought on to the campaign to "water the grassroots," utilizing "precinct-by-precinct networks that spew out voters on Election Day."[15] Merging these extant networks of social conservatives with the well-funded institutionalized politics of the Republican Party helped to jump-start the political infrastructure on the right before the 2004 campaign even began.

The Republican strategy was further enhanced by the party's 72-hour plan. This plan was explained to me by the political director of the 2004 Bush campaign, Terry Nelson: "Seventy-two hours is a bit of a misnomer, because [the plan] covers everything from absentee early voting, which is far outside the seventy-two-hour window, up to maximizing turnout on Election Day." Developed after the very tight presidential election of 2000, the Republican Party wanted to ensure that there were never again equal numbers of Republicans and Democrats at the polls. The plan created a systematic strategy for "contacting, motivating, and turning out every Republican and favorable Independent voter."[16] It was implemented by activating what Nelson referred to as a "volunteer army" to perform multiple tasks for the party.

In contrast to the Democrats, who had to determine the party's nominee through the primaries, which were not concluded until summer 2004, the Bush campaign started very early, organizing in target states in the summer and fall of 2003. Terry Nelson explained how the campaign developed a local infrastructure that would feed into the national campaign: "[We] put together our leadership teams, tried to identify our county chairs by the end of 2003, so we could begin to work on our precinct operation and just our general . . . organization . . . [It] was very much a ground-based campaign that was run with staff and headquarters and volunteer leaders, and county chairs and all that kind of stuff." In other words, because the party already had an infrastructure that connected the state party organizations to the national campaign and was already certain of its candidate, the Republicans were able to focus exclusively on developing local connections with party supporters who were firmly within its grassroots base.

The campaign also mobilized an historically Democratic demographic: young people. Using its knowledge of the youth evangelical movement that had sprung up on college campuses around the country, along with the increasing popularity of Christian Rock, the Bush campaign targeted young people who were likely to be supportive.[17] Youth outreach was run by the Bush campaign's national youth director, Jordan Sekulow. Whereas in 2000 it had begun its youth outreach only three months before the election, in 2004 the campaign started much earlier. Sekulow reported: "I came on fifteen months, sixteen months ahead of time to start organizing young people . . . While the Democrats were still battling in the primary, we were doing positive [campaigning] . . . and getting our grassroots involved and engaged very early . . . Our goal early on in the campaign was really to activate our students." Sekulow described the first youth outreach event, "Kick-off for Bush": "Our first event was at the Michigan–Ohio State game . . . two big [political] battlegrounds playing each other and, at that event, we had about a hundred and fifty students . . . Obviously, when you go to a college football game, you're reaching [out] to students."

Continuing to use college sporting events for youth outreach, the campaign created a large-scale program for signing up volunteers on the Students-for-Bush website: "Because [Students-for-Bush] launched in March, we used the March Madness [NCAA basketball tournament] . . . We set up a bracket system on-line where you could actually [compete] . . . just like in college basketball in the bracket system that was updated [in] real time." The competition focused on signing up volunteers in thirty-two states, including the battleground states. Sekulow explained how it worked:

> You could see if California was beating Florida in the third round of the bracket and [it] eventually got down to a championship game . . . We ended up, in just three weeks, with 21,000 more Students-for-Bush volunteers . . . We were over 50,000 students still well before the election and [the event] taught all of them how to get involved, how to get engaged . . . The two schools that won had over 2,000 students sign up in those three weeks.

In addition to capitalizing on popular collegiate sporting events, the Bush campaign reached out to young conservative Christians. Youth Director Sekulow, who is also an Evangelical Christian, reported how the Campaign reached out to Evangelical Christian organizations at schools, as well as pro-life and campus ministry groups. As a result of these many efforts to mobilize the conservative youth vote, Sekulow reported that their "numbers obviously went up" and that, by the end of the campaign, they had mobilized more than 128,000 student Bush volunteers.[18] While young people on the left were embroiled in the fight over who would become the Democratic nominee during the spring of 2004, the Bush campaign was identifying and mobilizing conservative young people around the country. As a result, it found itself armed with a corps of energetic young supporters in battleground states who had the free time to do whatever was needed to link the grassroots to the Republican Party's well-maintained political infrastructure.

Laying Sod versus Cultivating the Grass

The campaign strategies and political infrastructures of the Right and the Left mobilized and engaged their grassroots in very different ways. While the Republicans rallied local networks of conservatives to work for the campaign in swing states, the Democrats relied on paid professionals and imported volunteers from blue states to canvass and work for the campaign in swing and red states. Weighing in on the issue of political infrastructure, Karen Hicks, who worked as the national field director for the Democratic Party during the 2004 election after running Howard Dean's presidential campaign for the state of New Hampshire, tied the weakness of the Left to the way it connected with its grassroots base. In particular, she spoke about the Democrats' reliance on paid professionals to do the work of the campaign: "The trend within the Democratic Party has really been to outsource contact with voters to paid vendors and direct mail firms . . . [as well as] hiring people just to contact voters because it's a shortcut. It's a more reliable way to do it."

Josh Wachs from the DNC also hinted at the party's dependence on paid canvassers, calling them "paid volunteers" for the campaign. Payment for these "volunteers" took different forms. The Democratic strategy involved employing union members, including some laid-off steel workers, to work for the campaign.[19] An article in the *New York Times* also reported that the Service Employees International Union (SEIU) was working with ACT "to send as many as 2,000 members . . . [to] Ohio, Pennsylvania, and Florida to register and canvass voters. Starting this week [in April 2004], workers will take job leaves ranging from a few months to seven; ACT and the union will pay for lodging, transportation, a daily food allowance of $35 and a salary of $600 a week, slightly more than some now earn working in hospitals and nursing homes." For others, including students and unemployed people, 527 groups paid "$8 to $10 an hour to go door to door."[20] This type of paid volunteerism has been the norm in political organizing on the left for many years. Although it used to be an effective means of turning out enough urban voters to win campaigns, with the implementation of the 72-hour plan connecting localized networks of organized volunteers to the political infrastructure on the right, this strategy no longer seems sufficient.

Paying canvassers to go door to door ensures that the locals are contacted, but it does not engage the local institutions of civil society that have enduring roots in communities. Karen Hicks recognizes the limitation, noting that this type of political outsourcing "doesn't involve the longer-term work to develop grassroots capacity for people to organize in their own community . . . At the end of the campaign, you're left with nothing, basically, because all those canvassers walk out the door. It's not a job that most people do time and time again." After working on a campaign, most paid workers go back to their schools or jobs, or move on to an entirely different campaign, which is likely to be in a different place. Hicks, who got her start in politics as a paid canvasser, confirmed that my findings from the young people working for the People's Project were also true for other outsourced canvassers. In her experience with numerous Democratic campaigns, Hicks said that the people who canvassed for Democratic campaigns also tended to burn out quickly.[21] Hicks pondered how burning through paid canvassers in one election cycle affected the Democratic political infrastructure more broadly and concluded that the party ends up "starting over the next cycle with . . . no infrastructure developed." As a result of these problems, Hicks mused: "There's got to be a better way to not start from negative every single time."

Another reason that the Democrats were "starting from negative" was the effect such jobs have on the canvassers. Like the canvassers who worked for the People's Project, the paid canvassers who work on an electoral campaign come to the job with the desire to make a difference and tend to leave politics soon after the campaign ends. When asked how many of the people her firm had paid to go door to door during the 2004 campaign had stayed in politics, Laurie Moskowitz answered: "I think a small percentage of them . . . It's probably in the neighborhood of under 5 percent [who] actually go on to do anything of future significance." Of that 5 percent who may remain in politics past their first campaign, Moskowitz recognized that "there's a minuscule percentage that go on to have a long-term career in politics." Karen Hicks's experience of going from paid canvasser to long-term political operative was very unusual; most electoral canvassers are like the young people I met with the People's Project. Only a small handful of them found that canvassing changed their lives and directed them toward long-term political careers.

Even though canvassing led Hicks to pursue work in politics, she recognized the broader effects of a campaign that relies on paid work over volunteer work:

> The culture [in the Democratic Party] is [that I will] order up 15,000 "robo" [automated] calls 'cause I'm certain that they're gonna get made . . . [But] you don't transform people's lives by robo calls and paid canvassing [but] by helping them become . . . public leader[s] and helping them develop their skills, because leadership's not about having a checkbook big enough to pay your own way in politics . . . It's about developing really localized leadership and having everybody feel like they have a stake in public life.

With political organizing on the left tending to neglect the existing local institutions of civil society that could provide a lasting base for progressive politics, very few enduring connections remain at the local level after the campaigns are concluded that can be used in the next campaign cycle. Hiring people to do voter outreach and grassroots mobilization, instead of bringing in local volunteers during campaigns, has lasting effects on the Democratic Party's infrastructure (or lack thereof), as well as its base. For the infrastructure to support successful campaigns, the Democrats must put in the time and effort to reach the grassroots where the party's base lives, works, and votes, mobilizing people locally in a meaningful way.[22]

The consistency of professionalized political campaigns that rely predominantly on paid workers helps to explain the explosion of outsourced canvassing as a tactic for many national progressive groups. Even the Democratic Party outsourced its grassroots membership drive, hiring the for-profit group Grassroots Campaigns to train and coordinate paid canvassers to raise money. The purpose of hiring paid canvassers was to expand the financial base of the party. Josh Wachs summarized the effects of this outsourced canvassing: "We created hundreds of thousands of new grassroots donors, 90-some percent of which were new to the party . . . There were 700,000 new donors who were created through [it], which is really an incredible amount." Although this outsourced canvass recruited new supporters and was financially successful, disagreements arose over the politics of this type of outsourced fundraising. "They run very good canvass operations," a political consultant who worked on progressive grassroots outreach during the 2004 election said, but "they don't necessarily understand the state parties and the communication tools and how the DNC works." This lack of knowledge about how to work within the Democratic Party system caused some tension among party officials.

According to the Center for the Study of Elections and Democracy at Brigham Young University, other conflicts occurred within groups that hired canvassers to do electoral canvassing during the 2004 election. In a press release that compared the differences between the activities of 527 groups on the left and the right, the Center reported: "ACT and the America Votes coalition relied primarily on paid canvassers. In post-election hindsight, some concerns have been raised about the paid canvassing . . . [and the] negative feedback from MoveOn volunteers that worked in the ACT canvassing efforts and felt that the energy of the ACT paid canvassing effort was going in the wrong direction."[23]

In contrast to the programs that paid canvassers to do outreach, the programs that employed volunteers on the left were hampered by its limited political infrastructure. The party had no mechanism for plugging volunteers effectively into the campaign. Comparing the campaigns of the Right and the Left, Laurie Moskowitz said:

> The Republicans built a system that was based on personal connections over time . . . [They] had the time and energy invested in it, and the resources . . . to make sure that the people were connected and then [they] overlaid it with their national reporting, so that they knew what everybody was doing . . . You had your ten people . . . based on that personal connection. At the end of the day, we just were trying to make contacts. It was all we could do to build it in that short period of time.

As Moskowitz suggests, it is not that the Democrats were unable to mobilize volunteers. In fact, many who worked on the campaign reported mobilizing more Democratic volunteers than ever before. The real challenge to the Left was figuring out how to put these large numbers of volunteers to effective use. According to Josh Wachs: "The volunteer capacity was so huge, the issue [for us] was infrastructure capacity."

A relatively successful program was described by Joe Solmonese, the former chief executive officer of the progressive group EMILY's List, which rallied the members of what the group calls the "nation's largest grassroots political network" to volunteer.[24] Solmonese explained that this leading political action committee for pro-choice women candidates had historically spent its money hiring paid canvassers:

> For many years at these national organizations . . . , you'd get people who would say "I'm going to give you $1,000." You'd go to them and you'd say . . . "We have a big campaign coming up in Chicago. You live in Chicago . . . [and] we'd love you to go the next three Saturdays to canvass for us." And these women would say . . . "I'll give you $5,000 if I don't have to do that. Go pay more people to do it." For a long time, EMILY's List would say "OK, we'll take that $5,000 and go hire canvassers."

More recently, however, the group became less willing to hire canvassers to do grassroots outreach. Instead, EMILY's List started insisting that its donors do more than just contribute money. Solmonese continued:

> These women who years ago would say, "I don't want any part of it, I'll just give you money," they're now starting to say "I will canvass. If that's what it takes, I'll do it." . . . They're seeing that that's what happens on the other side: everybody works. Rich, poor, no matter what, you work. There is a field infrastructure of life [on the right]. It's not just about people giving a lot of money.

In his experience running progressive groups that have worked on issues related to abortion (EMILY's List) and same-sex marriage (the Human Rights Campaign), Solmonese had witnessed how differently the Right and the Left organize their political bases.[25] In order to compete with the Right, he recognized the need to mobilize his donors to do *more* than contribute money.

In addition, because of the complaints about the ACT canvasses, the MoveOn Political Action Committee decided to create a "Leave No Voter Behind" voter mobilization effort that relied entirely on local volunteers.[26] The goal of this neighbor-to-neighbor program was to get volunteers to "take responsibility for staying in contact with a group of targeted local voters in their neighborhood" for the last few days before the election.[27] Although this program, which was independent of the 527-sponsored voter outreach programs, started late, it reported mobilizing 70,000 volunteers who contacted unlikely voters in 10,000 precincts.[28]

One of the major ways that the Left mobilized volunteers during the 2004 election was to import them from blue states to work in battleground areas. Although both sides reported busing in people to do voter outreach, the Democrats boasted that their program was much larger. Josh Wachs explained that the Left would "send you to a place that's needed . . . I think there's no question [that the Right] didn't have a program like we did . . . from the party perspective . . . of moving people around into target states from nontarget states." Mobilizing progressive volunteers who are not grounded in the localities and places where they work ignored existing personal bonds among like-minded Democrats. It was, in essence, throwing bodies at a problem that required friends and neighbors.

When I asked Wachs if he thought that this importation of nonlocals could have had a negative effect on the outcome of the campaign, he dismissed the idea: "The argument has been overstated. In every swing and target state, we had a larger base of local volunteers than we ever had before. In many cases, they were supplemented by a huge number of volunteers from around the country." Tom Lindenfeld, who worked with the "giant turnout machine" ACT,[29] agreed: "This myth that . . . [the Republicans'] operation was more capable or impactful because it was based on workers who were local and they were volunteers, as compared to ours who were brought in from other places and perhaps were paid, that's a myth of a sort that doesn't compute."

Although these influential political operatives were skeptical of such a critique, others were not. Karen Hicks, for example, who coordinated the Dean campaign in New Hampshire, talked about the campaign's decision to bring in nonlocals to work the field before the primary in Iowa: "The last thing I would want in a state is to [bring in] 2,000 people from somewhere else." Besides importing volunteers from other states, the campaign coordinators in Iowa decided to make their workers visibly identifiable, dressing everyone from the Dean campaign in identical campaign hats. Hicks continued, "Putting an orange hat on them so that you can pick them out six miles away . . . it was just . . . the antithesis of what you want. You want somebody that you know, or somebody who looks like you to talk to you." In short, Hicks believed that the practices in Iowa drew attention to how few campaign workers were indigenous to the state in which they were working.

The Club for Growth, a fiscally conservative 527 group, capitalized on this aspect of the Dean campaign in a television advertisement that premiered in Iowa media markets on January 7, 2004. Aimed at criticizing the Dean campaign, the commercial received attention around the country. The Dean for America website printed a synopsis:

> The ad features a husband and wife and opens with an announcer asking, "What do you think about Howard Dean's proposal to raise your taxes by $1,900 a year?"
>
> The husband replies, "Well, I think Howard Dean should take his tax-hiking, government-expanding, latte-drinking, sushi-eating, Volvo-driving, *New York Times*–reading . . . "
>
> The wife jumps in: " . . . body-piercing, Hollywood-loving, left-wing freak show back to Vermont where it belongs."[30]

This tactic of importing campaign workers from out-of-state and then identifying them backfired for the Dean campaign. Instead of making the campaign look strong, it accentuated the fact that the campaign was not using local people who were grounded in the communities in which they were doing outreach. In addition, it gave groups on the right an easy target.

The importation of nonlocal volunteers became less visibly apparent to the broader American public after the primaries, but the practice continued on the left throughout the election. Josh Wachs summarized the DNC's "Road Trippers Program," which brought in nonlocals to work in swing states and contributed an estimated 25,000 people days to the campaign: "If you had anywhere from three days to three months that you're willing to give . . . we help coordinate housing, we send you to a place that's needed . . . We had a [paid] staff of twelve people . . . who just did that in the final three months of the campaign."

The potential problems associated with importing nonlocal campaign workers resonated with many progressive groups after the 2004 election ended. Sally Green Heaven, the deputy field director of the Human Rights Campaign, for example, invoked Tip O'Neill's famous motto: "I came out of the 2004 election believing one thing very strongly, and it's that all politics really is local and all grassroots organizing really is local. It's time-intensive and it's face-to-face . . . and it's real." Moreover, "If you want to get anything done on the local level, on the grassroots level . . . [you need] someone who lives there and isn't just like an operative that we dropped there . . . from San Francisco."

In contrast to the Left's campaign, which relied predominantly on outsourced paid professionals and imported volunteers, the Bush campaign capitalized on the existing connections of intermediary civic institutions. It identified the party's natural constituencies, which included religious conservatives, hunting clubs, and veterans' groups, and set out to mobilize them. Through the GOP's sophisticated 72-hour plan, Republicans funneled church members and other socially conservative citizens into a pyramid of Republican volunteer activists around the country.

The Bush campaign's political director, Terry Nelson, explained the grassroots aspects of the plan: "We started out the campaign always wanting to mobilize and try to have a volunteer army that was mobilized on our behalf . . . We asked our volunteers to sign up other volunteers on their own . . . to ask them to become part of the campaign and part of the volunteer organization and then people would come in." The underlying philosophy of the plan was based on shared norms.[31] In Nelson's words: "Individuals who share a common set of beliefs, values, and backgrounds talking with other individuals can be an effective form of communication and persuasion." The Bush campaign believed that the most effective way to mobilize sympathetic voters was to rally them to contact people they already knew. The campaign identified reliable voters (those who tended to vote in every election) and encouraged them to motivate their less reliable friends and neighbors who happened to have similar beliefs.

This model of identifying and mobilizing like-minded individuals to serve as campaign volunteers was further enhanced by the Bush campaign's outreach to so-called *conservative coalitions*. Gary Marx, who served as the National Conservative Coalition's director for the Bush campaign, explained how he mobilized economic and social conservatives by working through each individual's "sphere of influence." Following the pyramid structure of the Republican Party's infrastructure, Marx summarized their strategy: asking volunteers to "e-mail their friends and family [and] to send postcards out . . . [through the resources available on the campaign's] website." The 72-hour plan outlined key activities that included: voter registration; voter identification; direct contact and advocacy with absentee voters; a face-to-face push to encourage voters to vote early; mailing, calling, and canvassing Republicans; [and] canvassing, mailing, and calling Independent voters. [32] Through the campaign's website, volunteers could learn how to participate in these activities and how to implement the plan.

To motivate its volunteers to drum up the people within their spheres of influence, the campaign rewarded its most successful volunteers. The Bush Team Leaders (B.T.L.'s) were given prizes, "like a signed note from the President, for accomplishing six specific tasks, the first of which is to recruit five other B.T.L.'s. Volunteers are also rewarded . . . for calling in to talk radio programs or writing letters to the editor on behalf of the President." [33] The campaign eventually decided against using the term "team leader." Its political director explained: "It actually was something that discouraged people . . . There are people out there who don't want to be leaders . . . We thought of the program more as our basic volunteer program and we ended up reframing it as Bush volunteers and dropping the team leader concept." The campaign did, however, continue to provide motivational rewards for its volunteers, including coffee mugs, mouse pads, and personalized thank you letters. In some cases, people who had served as what the campaign's National Conservative Coalition director called "key volunteer leaders" received larger tokens of appreciation, such as invitations to the inauguration.

Rewards were also given to schools that won the Students-for-Bush competition during the NCAA basketball tournament. The Bush campaign's national youth director explained that the winners "got a basketball signed by the president as well as . . . a special conference call." In addition, the students were told that the campaign would use the numbers of volunteers at each school to determine where the president would go during his visits to battleground states. The executive director of the DNC during the 2004 campaign, Josh Wachs, recognized that it was much easier for the Republicans to provide such rewards because their candidate was already in the White House: they "had an extensive system of carrots and sticks."

In the end, the Bush campaign's 72-hour plan was very successful in recruiting volunteers. Although he was unable to provide specific numbers, Nelson reported:

> We had a goal for the number of Bush volunteers we were trying to achieve. That goal was based on one Bush volunteer for every fifty Bush voters, which was based on our vote goal for the state, for the county, and for the precinct. We had that broken down all the way to the precinct level, so if there were 250 Bush voters in the precinct, then we would want to have five Bush volunteers there to help organize that precinct. What I can tell you is that two times we revised the goal upwards. We exceeded the goal in every state [and] in every target state.

Although some political consultants on the left challenged the effectiveness of the 72-hour plan, others recognized its strength. Tom Lindenfeld was skeptical. He explained that, on the night of the election, he drove with *New York Times Magazine* writer Matt Bai to look for the 72-hour plan volunteers in action. During his drive around exurban Ohio, he was unable to see the voter turnout that the Republicans had boasted about and that Bai wrote about in his article. In addition, Lindenfeld reported that his post-election research on rural and exurban people from Ohio did not support Republican claims about the strength of the 72-hour plan.[34] He said he did not find people who voted because of their contact with neighbors or through their churches and that he was "enormously dubious about [the effectiveness of the 72-hour plan] . . . It's not possible to operate and not be seen."

Other political operatives on the left, however, were not surprised by the lack of visible turnout; they did not expect the 72-hour plan to be as visible as the Democratic model, which had canvassers going door-to-door on Election Day and people standing on streetcorners around voting areas with signs. Laurie Moskowitz explained: "I actually think it's highly possible not to see [the people doing outreach on the right] because they weren't out on the street, they were having conversations with neighbors and colleagues—people who live in their communities. They didn't need to go on the street, because they were talking to people in the house right next door."

In his post-election follow-up article, Matt Bai corroborated this perspective: "In shiny new town-house communities, canvassing could be done quietly by neighbors; you didn't need vans and pagers." In contrast to canvassing operations like the People's Project, which drops young people in neighborhoods to walk door to door with clipboards, the 72-hour plan mobilized local people *already* living in those neighborhoods to communicate with people they already knew. Through the 72-hour plan, the Republicans successfully increased voter turnout in the exurban precincts of Ohio by 68 percent.[35]

In the end, it is clear that the continued reliance on professional organizers, paid campaign workers, and imported volunteers to mobilize Democratic voters was less effective than a volunteer system that depended on local people who were already connected through local civil society groups. Getting a phone call from your church friend Bob, or a visit from Betty the next-door neighbor, is more likely to mobilize a sympathetic vote than a college student who comes to town only to work on the campaign: Bob will be at the church picnic on Sunday, and Betty will be available to watch the kids the next time you need a babysitter.

Chapter 6

Where Do We Go from Here?

The Future of Grassroots Politics in America

A t the heart of this book is the question: what is the role of citizens in democracy in America? Witnessing the Right as they harness social capital and the "norms of reciprocity and trustworthiness" among like-minded Americans,[1] it is impossible not to see the difference such meaningful participation makes in our political institutions and our democracy more broadly. The Republican Party used its 72-hour plan to capitalize on its extensive political infrastructure, reaching out to American communities to identify voters who are connected through personal social networks at the grassroots level. As I have illustrated throughout this book, it is misguided to assume that hiring people to knock on doors, stand on streetcorners, and make phone calls can strengthen a failing or nonexistent political infrastructure on the left. Given the results of my research on canvassers working for the People's Project, hiring paid workers to perform the job of grassroots outreach may even be doing more harm than good.

Rethinking Canvassing in America

When I last met with my former student Laura, I asked if she could see herself working in politics in the future. After experiencing a year out in the "real world," she responded: "Over time, I've realized that everything you do is political . . . I really believe that now." Although she told me she would consider working on another electoral campaign, Laura asked me to write her a recommendation for law school. In the near future, I expect to see Laura leaving politics for graduate school and then moving on to a job that values her skill and enthusiasm and engages her more fully.

Based on my research on summer canvassers who worked for the People's Project in 2003, I doubt that many of them will be as resilient as Laura. While the most ambitious and creative young people on the right are being groomed for more powerful roles in politics via a party machine that assesses each individual's potential and determines the best way to capitalize on their personal strengths to help the conservative cause,[2] motivated young people on the left have fewer and fewer opportunities to participate in politics. One of the remaining options that yields a paycheck is working for the People's Project.

In order to recruit and retain large numbers of members for progressive organizations, the People's Project employs idealistic young people who are looking for opportunities in progressive politics during their summer vacations from college and after graduation. For most canvassers, the Project represents their introduction to politics in America. But the relationship is one-sided, all consuming, and exhausting, so much so that the People's Project assumes most canvassers will not last very long—and they don't. Therefore, the Project has developed a standardized model to train them quickly and get them out on the streets as soon as possible raising money for their causes. Given the Project's constraints, using such a model makes sense and has successfully raised money and increased membership for many progressive groups so that they can continue their work.

But in contrast to the well-funded conservative organizations on the right, the groups on the left have become caught in a self-perpetuating trap that relies on a model of grassroots activism that also has serious unintended consequences. It is this system of grassroots outreach that is contributing to the crisis of progressive politics in America today.

The standardized model was designed to guarantee identical results no matter who is doing the canvassing; as such, it ensures that progressive groups will continue to have funding and members. At the same time, it assumes that these idealistic young people have nothing beyond their time and their bodies to add to progressive campaigns. During the summer of 2003, this machine generated a grassroots membership base for campaigns to clean up rivers, limit logging in old-growth forests, support alternative energy, curtail urban sprawl, safeguard the Clean Air Act, support impoverished youth, and prevent hate crimes. Even though the goal of each campaign was different, the process that the Project used to reach its objectives around the country was the same: sending canvassers out to recruit members and raise funds. In a model that treats canvassers as replaceable cogs in a well-oiled machine, where every aspect of the campaign is scripted, including the words the canvassers are required to say at the doors and on the streets, some young people will fit better than others.

Those who are comfortable with this model include gregarious young people who are willing to talk to strangers about campaigns and organizations about which they have limited knowledge. Successful directors for campaign offices know that participating in progressive politics requires that they work long hours, be willing to sacrifice their personal lives for the cause, and go wherever the organization needs them. The many who do not fit the model include those who are not comfortable speaking to strangers and selling political campaigns as if they were encyclopedias. A number of canvassers who decided to leave were more interested in asking questions and deliberating about the best solutions to political problems than reciting a script; they wanted to be involved in the hard work of democracy.[3]

There are broad and important effects of this model on progressive politics in America: it does not leave room for innovation within grassroots campaigns, it turns off the concerned young people who were motivated enough to try out canvassing in the first place, and sometimes it hands victory to the other side. In addition, with the consolidation of canvassing, understanding the effects of this strategy on maintaining a grassroots base matters more than ever, since working within this model is the ticket for young people into progressive politics today.

One effect of the consolidation of grassroots activism is that many entry-level jobs in progressive politics now involve canvassing. The Project partners with several programs for college graduates, all of which include three months of canvass-directing during the summer. Although the People's Project sees itself as a training ground for future progressive leaders, only successful canvassers can be successful in the organization and take advantage of the Project's contacts with progressive groups. Young people take the jobs to make a difference, but too many get turned off or spit out by a standardized system that measures political change and success in terms of money and nominal membership over progress and movement toward political goals.

Almost all of the canvassers I met during the summer of 2003 felt happy with their work as paid activists after having worked for the Project for only a few weeks.[4] By the time I spoke with them a year later, however, too many had become disillusioned with both canvassing and politics more broadly. Even though the progressive movement needs idealistic young people, many are turned away. To be sure, some survive and work their way through the ranks of organizations like the People's Project. But because their introduction to politics was through outsourced canvassing, too many progressive young people end up leaving politics forever.

The consolidation of progressive politics also increases the distance between national progressive groups and their members. As civic and political organizations have become increasingly professionalized, the ways that they engage their members have become less personal. Most national progressive groups do not require any actual participation from their members beyond writing checks. As Harry Boyte points out: "Politics has largely become a spectator sport run by professionals with disdain for ordinary people."[5] This shift from *membership to management* has had serious consequences for the ways that Americans engage in politics and civic activity, particularly on the left.[6] It is important to remember that the outsourcing of grassroots campaigns and the proliferation of the standardized model for running such campaigns did not cause the problem. But, as so many progressive groups have closed down their independent grassroots offices and hired firms like the People's Project, they have become even less connected to their members. Under the watchful management of political professionals, young people working as paid canvassers and phone-bankers do the actual recruitment and fundraising. Often the people on the phones, on the streets, and at the doors have only limited knowledge of the organizations and campaigns on whose behalf they are working.

In other words, grassroots activism that relies on paid professionals to do the work of citizens is a shortcut that lets political groups avoid investing time and energy in building an infrastructure that would truly connect them with like-minded members. As the distance between national progressive groups and their members increases, the progressive agenda will lose more political battles and the options for progressive young people who want to work in politics will shrink even more.

For years, scholars have observed significant changes taking place in American politics, chief among them a growing disconnection between regular people and politics. With the professionalization of interest-oriented political groups, members have become more like consumers and less like engaged participants.[7] Members pay their dues, occasionally read their magazines, and sometimes even receive a canvas totebag. But this sort of passive participation cannot compete with campaigns that actually involve their members in meaningful ways.

With this study I have outlined how the outsourcing of progressive grassroots campaigns increases the distance between national progressive groups and their members while also contributing to the alienation of a generation of potential progressive leaders. This study of politics in America illustrates the mechanisms through which much of civic America has become disconnected from national politics on the left. One of the most surprising findings of this research is how differently the Right and the Left engage their members. These differences help to explain the failure of progressive politics in recent years.

Ironically, as ideologues continue debating the relationship between the state and civil society with those on the left describing civil society as a vital component of a strong welfare state and those on the right asserting that civil society should replace many of the functions of the state[8]—this study suggests that there has already been a resolution. In short, the local institutions of civil society are being harnessed by the Right to support the people in power. The Bush administration has been able to use this symbiotic relationship to further its agenda among the economic and ideological conservatives who constitute its voting base. Although Republicans such as former senator Dan Coats and Senator Rick Santorum claim "the most important civic renewal in our nation will take place entirely outside government,"[9] the Republican Party recognizes that the most effective political agendas and successful campaigns, like the

72-hour plan, connect local citizens and intermediary networks of civil society to the state through a mutually beneficial relationship.

Talking about a Revolution

It is important to remember that this system of grassroots outreach was originally formed to maintain member-supported interest groups that were an alternative to the "'predatory' system of party politics" at the turn of the twentieth century in the United States.[10] Over time, voluntary associations emerged that defined themselves by their members' interests—labor, agriculture, and even gender. These associations bypassed political parties and worked through the political system to lobby and advocate on behalf of their members. With the active participation of their members, these groups helped to advance the progressive agenda through the New Deal, and later during the 1960s.[11] With the innovation of canvassing in the 1970s, environmental and consumer interest groups were able to develop membership and funding bases that allowed them to engage in institutional politics as lobbyists and advocates. To maintain the funding and membership that makes such politics possible, outsourced canvassing has become the norm in progressive politics today. Unfortunately, this model for maintaining members merely reinforces the role of citizens as spectators.

As the Republicans continue to deepen their roots at the local level, the differences between how the Left and the Right engage their *members* becomes ever more important. Until the Left invests time and energy in creating a sustainable infrastructure that actually reaches down into communities in a meaningful way, future elections will likely continue to produce Republican victories. In close elections, progressive organizations will rely on the *man* and the *message*, while investing in expensive shortcuts that do not leave any lasting roots for the next election cycle. Without a committed and participatory membership among its constituency, political movements on the left have become overly reliant on scripted forms of political involvement that are top-down and one-sided. As a result, the *message* has changed from one that engages citizens as deliberative participants in the democratic process to one that treats them as consumers of sound bites who assert their political views primarily by writing checks. In addition, this reliance on quick fixes ends up fielding *men* and *women* to run for political office who are professional politicians. As such, they see voters as instruments for achieving specific goals and have no real connection to their fellow citizens.[12]

Although the Democratic Party has used these outsourcing tactics for years, it is becoming increasingly apparent that it cannot compete with political campaigns that truly engage local people and the local institutions of civil society. Political consultant Karen Hicks made this important point about the grassroots strategies embraced by the Left:

> At the end of the campaign, you're left with nothing . . . You don't transform people's lives by [outsourcing politics but] by helping them become . . . public leader[s] and helping them develop their skills, because leadership's not about having a checkbook big enough to pay your own way in politics . . . It's about developing really localized leadership and having everybody feel like they have a stake in public life.

For many Democratic political operatives, however, the 2004 election provided an entirely different lesson: more effort should go toward finding and supporting charismatic men and women candidates and making sure that they have a message that resonates with the people. If their prayers are answered, Hillary Clinton will emerge as the Democratic presidential candidate for the 2008 election. But relying on a charismatic candidate and crafting an infallible message will not solve the infrastructure problems of Democratic politics in America; nor will it reconnect the alienated Americans who are trying to understand what happened to the progressive agenda. In the words of former Democratic senator Bill Bradley: "Rebuilding civil society requires people talking and listening to each other, not blindly following a hero."[13] By implementing a shortcut that uses outsourced canvassers and imported volunteers, the Democratic Party does not create any grassroots capacity in local communities. This model is in stark contrast to the way the Right is mobilizing real networks of like-minded Americans and building an extensive political infrastructure that involves effective strategies for fundraising and paid professional mobilization.

After the 2004 presidential election, for example, many of the paid campaign professionals who were hired to canvass for the Democratic

Party and left-leaning 527 groups went back to their jobs and schools or moved on to other campaigns. The Republicans, in contrast, have transitioned many of their paid professionals into other political organizations on the right. In addition, and perhaps more important, the stable intermediary institutions that connected their *members* to the army of Bush volunteers continue to meet regularly to discuss how they can contribute to the political issues that concern them.

It is important to note, however, that progressive Americans *are* working successfully at the local level. Recent research has found numerous effective connections being made through civic innovation around the country.[14] But Americans who identify themselves as left-leaning are not being channeled into political discussions that connect them to national politics in a meaningful way. There are many local community groups in which progressive Americans are already *members*, including progressive book clubs; community-supported farms (CSA); cooperatives; environmental groups; lesbian, gay, bisexual, and transgender (LGBT) groups; park associations; women's rights groups; and all types of political organizations.[15] In addition, Americans today of all political leanings continue to be religiously engaged, but it is predominantly members of conservative Christian religious communities who have been mobilized by their friends and neighbors to participate in national politics.[16] The Bush campaign targeted specific "conservative coalitions" who were sympathetic to the campaign's platform. In a similar manner, left-leaning groups could harness the connections among progressive religious groups to tap into their "networks of reciprocity," but they have yet to build such a capacity.

Only through *meaningful membership* that involves conversations and lasting connections can social capital and social networks be harnessed to bring about political change. Like-minded progressive Americans have the ability to connect voters with similar values and mobilize them to participate politically, but creating a political infrastructure that links local groups to national political institutions takes time and commitment: it will require people at the national and grassroots levels working together to establish grassroots connections that are deep enough to bear fruit.

Research Methods Used in Data Collection and Comparing Canvassers to a National Sample

I n order to understand how young people experience working for a paid canvass, I studied one of the largest canvassing organizations in America, the People's Project, a pseudonym. (My data gathering agreement with the Project requires that it remain anonymous.) After negotiations with the People's Project, the Project granted me access to collect data at six regionally stratified, randomly selected canvasses around the United States. From a list of forty-one approved canvass offices nationwide, I drew the names of six from a hat—one in each region: Boulder, Colorado; Portland, Oregon; San Diego, California; Ann Arbor, Michigan; Baltimore, Maryland; and Atlanta, Georgia.

Methods Overview

I used a multi-stage approach to this study of activism in America. In the first stage, which took place during summer 2003, I collected both quantitative and qualitative data on canvassers who were working in the selected summer offices of the People's Project. During the second stage, beginning in May 2004, telephone interviews were conducted with members of the cohort of 2003 summer canvassers. At the end of the open-ended semi-structured phone interviews, the subjects were also asked follow-up survey questions. Table A1 lists the canvass offices studied and the number of canvassers interviewed at each stage of the study.

In addition, I interviewed representatives of national progressive groups and political consultants who worked for the Kerry and Bush campaigns during the 2004 presidential election. Data collection for all stages of this project was conducted in accordance with Columbia University's policies on research on human subjects (Columbia University IRB Proto-col #02/03-998A, IRB-AAAA0954, and IRB-AAAA3600).

All of the interviews were open-ended and semi-structured. The purpose of the semi-structured interviewing technique, as summarized by Lofland and Lofland, is "to achieve analyses that (1) are attuned to aspects of human group life, (2) depict aspects of that life, and (3) provide per-spectives on that life that are simply not available to or prompted by other methods of research."[1] The interviews and extensive notes and memos from all of the interviews were kept as part of the qualitative data set. I used a qualitative data analysis computer program (NVivo) to store, sort, and code transcribed data. As the patterns across cases emerged, I distinguished between first-order conclusions (those explicitly drawn or stated by the respondent), and second-order conclusions (those I drew from what was said). In so doing, I acknowledged my role in interpreting the data patterns, as well as in subjecting the respondents' claims to additional scrutiny.

Pseudonyms are used throughout this book to protect the privacy of those canvassers who shared their stories and of the representatives of the national office of the People's Project. When I refer to interviews with polit-ical consultants and representatives of national progressive groups who agreed to speak on the record, I provide their names and affiliations. For

Table A1. Canvass Offices and Number of Canvassers Interviewed in Each Location by Stage

Region	Office	Research period in 2003	Number of initial interviews on-site	Number of follow-up interviews
Northeast	Baltimore	Week of June 9	5	1
Southeast	Atlanta	Week of June 30	10	8
Northwest	Portland	Week of July 7	51	28
Midwest	Ann Arbor	Week of July 14	14	8
Southwest	Boulder	Week of July 21	22	8
California	San Diego	Week of July 28	13	9
Total			115	62

those people who spoke with me with the understanding that they would not be directly attributed, I give only their general affiliations. All of the quotations I include in this book have been edited to remove filler phrases and words such as "y'know, like, um, and kind of" that have no bearing on the content of the statements. In instances where these words provide additional meaning to the quotes, I did not delete them. Each stage of the data collection process is outlined in the next sections.

Stage 1: Surveying and Interviewing Canvassers

Throughout the summer of 2003, along with two graduate research assistants, I conducted participant observation of more than 200 young people being trained in organizing skills and educated about the issues that they would discuss with citizens at their doors and on the streets in six canvass offices. In accordance with my data gathering agreement with the People's Project, we formally interviewed 115 canvassers at the six regionally stratified randomly selected canvass offices around the United States.[2] Although the number of interviews varied by office, they included every canvasser in the office who was willing to participate and had completed the organization's requisite three-day training period. At the time of the first interview, most canvassers had not been working at the canvass for a significant time period. In fact, at the time of the initial interview for all of the canvassers in the sample who were not in administrative positions directing offices, the median was twenty days (the mean was thirty-four days).

In addition to the participant observation in each canvass office and the semi-structured open-ended interviews, all of the canvassers who participated in the interviews filled out a survey that was adapted from the 1996 National Household Education Survey (NHES) Civic Involvement Interviews; its purpose was to compare their levels of civic engagement with that of the general population. The NHES is a set of studies conducted by the U.S. Department of Education's National Center for Education Statistics, which are conducted on a nationally representative sample of adolescents and young adults.

The NHES is particularly well suited for such a comparison as it contains questions on several dimensions of civic engagement. Respondents were asked about their sources of information on government and national issues, civic participation, and knowledge and attitudes about government. In addition, the survey contains measures of opportunities youth have had to develop personal responsibility and civic involvement. The most recent wave of the Youth Civic Engagement Component of the NHES was conducted in 1996. Although data were collected from 8,043 young people, in order to compare with the canvassers in this study—all of whom were at least 18 years old in the summer of 2003—only the data from the 384 participants in the youth component of the NHES who were 18 or older were included. Questions about socio-demographic status (e.g., age, race, family income, etc.) were also included in the adapted survey to gauge whether and how canvass participants differed in family background and demographic characteristics.

In the first stage of the study, all interviews included questions regarding the canvassers' motivations for joining the grassroots campaign and their impressions of the work. Each interview was based on the position and affiliation of the canvasser, and interviews lasted from twenty minutes to two hours. All interviews during this stage addressed the same range of topics:

1 *General background*: The educational and professional background of the person being interviewed.

2 *Personal motivation for participation in the summer canvass*: The interviewee's personal motivation for joining the summer canvass and his or her interpretation of the reasons why young people join the summer canvass (when applicable).

3 *Interpretation of the goals and efficacy of the summer canvass*: The perceptions of the interviewee based on his or her experience.

4 *Effects of the summer canvass on personal level of civic engagement*: The interviewee's opinion regarding the effect of the canvassing experience on his or her personal political and civic involvement.

5 *Future intentions*: The interviewee's intentions regarding how long she or he will work for the canvass and what she or he plans to do if and when she or he leaves.

Stage 2: Follow-up Interviews and Surveys

From May to November 2004, follow-up telephone interviews were conducted with the sample of 2003 summer canvassers. In these interviews, members of the 2003 cohort of summer canvassers were asked about their current levels of civic engagement and to reflect on their experiences with the canvass. Canvassers were also asked how long had they worked for the canvass and, if they had left, why they left and what they did afterward. About 14 percent of the canvassers from this cohort were still working for the People's Project when I followed up with them in 2004. Of those canvassers who were not directors, the median length of their working for the People's Project was eleven weeks (the mean was twenty weeks). Exactly half of the canvassers who were part of the original sample participated in the follow-up component of the study, and approximately 56 percent of the canvass directors participated.[3] Given the follow-up component's response rate of approximately 60 percent,[4] it is likely that these data are biased toward those who continued to work for the organization.

At the end of the follow-up interview, we asked additional survey questions that were adapted from the NHES. These questions involved the types of civic and political activities that the interviewee might have participated in in the past year, including voting and volunteering. In the final section of this Appendix, I present a summary of these findings in comparison with data from the NHES.

Stage 3: Studying Representatives of National Progressive Groups and Political Consultants

In the spring and summer of 2005, I interviewed representatives of national progressive groups that had outsourced to the People's Project in order to understand their grassroots strategies and tactics. I contacted all of the groups that were listed on the Project's website as clients in May 2005 and requested a meeting with a representative who was responsible for that particular group's grassroots outreach.[5] I interviewed representatives from six of those groups in Washington, D.C., in May 2005. I asked them to describe the work that their group does at the grassroots level and how they engage with their members—how frequently and with what types of interaction.

I also interviewed political consultants on the left and the right in order to understand better the grassroots strategies adopted by the Bush and Kerry campaigns. Beginning with each campaign's website and media accounts of the grassroots mobilization for each campaign, using a snowball sampling procedure I identified consultants whose work specifically pertained to each campaign's grassroots outreach. During interviews, I asked them about the type of work they did in the 2004 campaign, the organizations with whom they worked, the ways that their organization (or section of the campaign) aimed to mobilize the grassroots, and how they specifically targeted young people to participate in the campaign.

Finally, I interviewed the two men who have been credited with creating some of the most prominent national canvassing groups, Marc Anderson and David Zwick. I asked both of them to provide a history of their experiences canvassing and the organizations with which they were involved.

Comparing Canvassers to a National Sample

Most of the canvassers were politically progressive, but had yet to get involved in politics. In contrast to the engaged young people that Sabrina Oesterle and her colleagues find to have been involved since high school,[6] this cohort of canvassers was only just starting to become civically engaged. In comparison to a national sample from the National Household Education Survey (NHES), however, the canvassers were much more knowledgeable about the American political process and were significantly more civic-minded.[7] Table A2 presents a comparison between the canvassers and the national average.

Of the participants in the follow-up interviews, only a small percentage were still working for the canvass in 2004. Although participation in the canvass after one year was less than expected given their intentions in summer 2003, these young people continued to be civically engaged. Canvassers were significantly more politically knowledgeable than the young people surveyed in the national sample. The "political knowledge aggregate" variable sums the correct responses from the following questions: Whose responsibility is it to determine if a law is constitutional or not . . . is it the president, the Congress, or the Supreme Court? Which party now has the most members in the House of Representatives in Washington? How much of a majority is required for the U.S. Senate and House to override a presidential veto? Which of the two major parties is more conservative at the national level? In addition, the canvassers were much more civically aware. The "civic awareness aggregate" variable was created by summing the correct responses to whether the canvasser had heard of a number of national civic programs: the Peace Corps, VISTA, and AmeriCorps. Finally, in a comparison with an aggregate variable of civic and political action the difference between the means of the two samples was statistically significant. The "civic and political action aggregate" variable was created to measure this concept by combining the responses from eight questions about the respondents' civic and political activity over the previous twelve months. Topics covered ranged from civic activity to politics: e.g., Do you participate in any ongoing community service activity,

Table A2. Answers to Selected Questions by the NHES Sample and Canvassers

Question	National sample	Canvassers
Whose responsibility is it to determine if a law is constitutional or not... is it the president, the Congress, or the Supreme Court? (% correct)	49	88
Which party now has the most members in the House of Representatives in Washington? (% correct)	48	91
How much of a majority is required for the U.S. Senate and House to override a presidential veto? (% correct)	34	46
Which of the two major parties is more conservative at the national level? (% correct)	44	94
Have you ever heard of the Peace Corps? (% yes)	81	100
Have you ever heard of VISTA? (% yes)	26	56
Have you ever heard of AmeriCorps? (% yes)	38	95
Do you read the news daily (% yes)	17	33
Do you talks about politics daily (% yes)	6	66

NOTE: Percentages are rounded to the nearest full percentage point.

Table A3. Comparison of Means between the NHES Sample and
             Canvassers for Selected Variables

Variable	t-statistic	Significance
How often reads the news	3.926	.000
How often talks about politics	14.169	.000
Political knowledge aggregate	7.422	.000
Civic awareness aggregate	10.104	.000
Civic and political action aggregate	11.660	.000

NOTE: Based on the results of Levene's Test for Equality of Variance, all statistics were
calculated with equal variances assumed.

for example, volunteering at a school, coaching a sports team, or working
with a church or neighborhood association? In the past twelve months,
have you contributed money to a candidate, a political party, or some
political cause? And, in the past twelve months, have you participated in
a protest or boycott? Table A3 presents the results of the comparison of
means between the two samples.

Notes

Notes to Preface

1. Personal communication with the author September 17, 2005.

2. My data gathering agreement with this organization requires that its identity remain anonymous. Throughout the book I refer to it as "the People's Project" or "the Project."

3. For details about my research methods, see the Appendix to this book.

4. Follow-up interviews were conducted with approximately two-thirds of the canvassers who agreed to be contacted for a follow-up interview and provided contact information.

Notes to Chapter 1

1. For more information about Locks of Love, see www.locksoflove.org (accessed September 8, 2005).

2. See, for example, Laurie Goodstein and David D. Kirkpatrick, "On a Christian Mission to the Top: Evangelicals Set Their Sights on the Ivy League," *New York Times*, May 22, 2005, p. A1; Jeff Horwitz,"My Right-Wing Degree," Salon.com, May 25, 2005; Hanna Rosin, "God and Country: A College That Trains Young Christians to Be Politicians," *New Yorker*, June 27, 2005.

3. America Coming Together was a left-leaning 527 political group that aimed to "organize, inform, and empower voters" around the 2004 election. The organization was shut down in August 2005 (www.acthere.com [accessed February 25, 2006]).

4. Farhad Manjoo, "Why Bush Won," Salon.com, November 4, 2004; Matthew Rothschild, "Kerry, How Dare You!" *The Progressive*, November 3, 2004.

5. markschmitt.typepad.com/decembrist/2004_elections/index.html (accessed July 21, 2005).

6. See, for example, "The 2000 Elections State by State," *New York Times*, November 9, 2000, p. B15.

7. Bill Bradley, "A Party Inverted," *New York Times*, March 30, 2005, p. 17.

8. Blake Morrison, "Dean Scream Gaining Cult-Like Status on Web," *USA Today*, January 22, 2004. For a full listing of these remixes, see http://politicalhumor.about.com/b/a/059035.htm (accessed November 21, 2005).

9. See, for example, Alan Cooperman, "Same-Sex Bans Fuel Conservative Agenda," *Washington Post*, November 4, 2004, p. A39; Dana Milbank, "Deeply Divided Country Is United in Anxiety," *Washington Post*, November 4, 2004, p. A28; Todd S. Purdum, "An Electoral Affirmation of Shared Values," *New York Times*, November 4, 2004, p. A1; and Katharine Q. Seelye, "Moral Values Cited as a Deciding Issue of the Election," *New York Times*, November 4, 2004, p. 4. But see David Brooks, "The Values-Vote Myth," *New York Times*, November 6, 2004, p. 19.

10. Frank (2004, pp. 258–59).

11. Lindenfeld, interview with the author, May 2005.

12. Lakoff (2004). For a discussion of Lakoff's contribution to democratic framing, see also Matt Bai, "The Framing Wars." *New York Times Magazine*, July 17, 2005, pp. 38–45.

13. Joyce Purnick, "One-Doorbell-One-Vote Tactic Re-emerges in Bush-Kerry Race: Foraging for Votes," *New York Times*, April 6, 2004, p. A1.

14. The importance of the voting base was emphasized by some media outlets right after the election. See, for example, Julia Duin, "GOP Tells of Success Wooing Catholic Vote," *Washington Times*, November 5, 2004, p. A04; William Glanz, "Unions' All-Out Effort Comes Up Short," *Washington Times*, November 4, 2004, p. C10. See also Joan Vennochi, "Was Gay Marriage Kerry's Undoing?" *Boston Globe*, November 4, 2004, p. A15.

15. See, for example, Matt Bai, "Machine Dreams: America Coming Together Is History—along with Any Idea of a Top-Down Political Party," *New York Times Magazine*, August 21, 2005, pp. 11–12.

16. See particularly Tocqueville (1876/1966). See also Almond and Verba (1963). For more recent comparisons, see Ladd (1999); Schofer and Fourcade-Gourinchas (2001); and Wuthnow (1991).

17. See Putnam (2000, p. 402); see also Putnam (1995, 1996).

18. See Bellah et al. (1995). These findings have been corroborated by other scholars as well; see, for example, Levine and Lopez (2002); Nie, Verba, and Petrocik (1979); Eliasoph (1998); Piven and Cloward (1988, 2000); Reiter (1979); Verba, Schlozman, and Brady (1995). For contrasting views, see Lichterman (1996); Paxton (1999); and Rotolo (1999).

19. Skocpol (1999, p. 499, emphasis in original). On how Americans engage, see also Boyte and Kari (1996); Eckstein (2001); Ladd (1999); McDonald and Popkin (2001); Wuthnow (1994, 1998). On changes in the types of engagement, see Skocpol (2003, 1996); Skocpol, Ganz, and Munson (2000).

20. This innovation was made possible by recent advancements in communication technologies. Before the Internet, most mail-in members had very limited opportunities to participate in the campaigns of national advocacy groups that they supported.

21. Since 1998 this group has expanded to include what its website calls a "family of organizations." See www.moveon.org for more information (accessed August 3, 2005).

22. See, for example, Elizabeth Bernstein,"Katrina Prompts Record Pace of Giving." *Wall Street Journal*, September 6, 2005, p. D1.

23. For a full discussion of symbolic politics, see Edelman (1964).

24. See Berry (1999, p. 389); see also Berry (1997).

25. See Clemens (1997, p. 320).

26. Weir and Ganz (1997, p. 150). See also Schlozman and Tierney (1986) and Walker (1991).

27. Fiorina (1999, p. 416).

28. In my definition of the Right, I include both economic and ideological conservatives. For a recent history, see Balz and Brownstein (1996).

29. For more information about the Christian Coalition, see www. cc.org/about.cfm (accessed August 3, 2005). See also the timeline provided on Theocracy Watch, which is sponsored by the Center for Religion, Ethics and Social Policy (CRESP) at Cornell University (see www.theocracywatch. org/taking_over.htm [accessed August 3, 2005]).

In fact, Ralph Reed, the Christian Coalition's former political director, has become so mainstream in the Republican Party that he chaired the Southeast Region for Bush-Cheney '04 and served as the party's campaign manager for the state of Georgia. Scholars such as Weir and Ganz (1997) have linked the development of this network of grassroots connections on the right to the end of the Goldwater campaign in 1964. For a profile of Ralph

Reed and the development of the Christian Coalition, see "Fighting for God and the Right Wing," *Time*, September 13, 1993, p. 58.

30. See Greg Goldin, "The 15 Per Cent Solution: How the Christian Right Is Building from Below to Take Over from Above," *Village Voice*, April 6, 1993, pp. 19–21.

31. See Matt Bai, "The Mulilevel Marketing of the President," *New York Times Magazine*, April 25, 2004, p. 43.

32. Rod Martin, "Quiet Revolution: The Christianization of the Republican Party," *The Christian Statesman* (www.natreformassn.org/statesman/02/chrepub.html [accessed August 5 2005]).

33. Rosin, "God and Country"; see also Goodstein and Kirkpatrick, "On a Christian Mission to the Top."

34. Data available from the Fourth National Survey on Religion and Politics. For more information, see Green (2004).

35. Harry C. Boyte, "A Tale of Two Playgrounds," paper presented at the American Political Science Association meetings in San Francisco, 2001, p. 3; see also Boyte, Booth, and Max (1986).

36. Green (2004, p. 23). For an overview of the research on canvassing, see Bartell and Bouxsein (1973); Green, Gerber, and Nickerson (2003); Huckfeldt and Sprague (1992). See also Green and Gerber (2004, chap. 3); and Morlan (1955).

37. For a full discussion, see McAdam (1988).

38. In addition to canvassing, volunteers aided the respective campaigns by working phone banks and participating in visibility events.

39. See www.hbay.com/ (accessed September 12, 2005).

40. For a full account of this movement, see Morlan (1955).

41. The original name of Clean Water Action was Fishermen's Clean Water Action Project.

42. Boyte, Booth, and Max (1986, p. 81).

43. Keeter et al. (2002). Because most canvassing offices require canvassers to be 18 or older, it is likely that this percentage *underestimates* the participation of the general population.

44. Interest in and funding for progressive causes commonly decreases during a Democratic presidency. For a discussion of such political cycles, see Dunlap and Catton (1994). On the decline of grassroots outreach, see, for example, John B. Judis, "Activist Trouble," *American Prospect* (January 1998) (www.prospect.org/print-friendly/print/V9/36/judis-j.html [accessed March 7, 2006]).

45. Sirianni and Friedland (2001, pp. 8, 9, emphasis in original); see also Boyte (2004).

46. My data gathering agreement with this organization requires that its identity remain anonymous. Throughout the book I refer to it as "the People's Project" or "the Project."

47. This number is based on estimates from a representative at the national office. The exact number of campaign offices varies from year to year.

48. www.grassrootscampaigns.com/about.html (accessed, May 13, 2004).

Notes to Chapter 2

1. Like the names of all canvassers in this book, Jerry is a pseudonym.

2. Some offices run more than one shift of street canvassers a day. The Boulder canvass office, for example, ran two shifts: one during business hours and one later in the day on Pearl Street, where street performers entertain crowds each evening.

3. Canvassers in different offices recalled different numbers of briefings at different times. Members of the Boulder canvass recalled having the most: at least one briefing a week at the beginning of the summer.

4. Trainers were responsible for training new canvassers, and field managers were responsible for managing the teams while they were out canvassing. It is worth noting that a number of those who were asked to become field managers reported declining. Some explained that they were uncomfortable with the greater time commitment, which did not come with a proportionate increase in remuneration.

5. Clemens (1997, p. 318).

6. These issues were mentioned during the summer of 2003 and in follow-up interviews in 2004.

7. Ben Ehrenreich, "Busting Unions: Progressives Can Do It Too," *LA Weekly*, February 6, 2002, www.laweekly.com/ink/02/12/news-ehrenreich.php (accessed July 5, 2005).

8. The *Student Underground* is "a not-for-profit, student run, democratic collective, based at Boston University." For more information, see www.thestudentunderground.org/staff.php3 (accessed September 15, 2005).

9. Valerie Costa, "Practice What You Preach!" *Student Underground*, www.thestudentunderground.org/print.php3?ArticleID=163 (accessed July 5, 2005).

10. On Wal-Mart, see, for example, Ortega (1998); see also Liza Featherstone, "Is Union-Busting Bad for Business?" *The Nation*, May 23, 2005, www.thenationlcom/doc/20050523/featherstone (accessed March 7, 2006).

11. Canvassers around the country reported similar numbers of hours.

12. I heard these accounts about directors in Baltimore, Atlanta, Minneapolis, and California.

13. This estimate is based on the number of canvass directors I was able to reach for follow-up interviews in 2004. For those directors whose e-mail accounts with the organization had been closed, it is likely that they had left. Although I was able to track down two directors who had left the organization through alternative contact information, many were unreachable.

14. See Putnam (1995, 1996); see also Bourdieu (1986); Coleman (1988); Edwards and Foley (1998); Minkoff (1997); Paxton (2002); and Portes (1998).

Notes to Chapter 3

1. www.idealist.org/about/mission.html (accessed June 8, 2005).

2. As Paul Lichterman found in his study of environmental activist groups, these canvassers were driven, not by their personal connections or commitment to traditional values, but by their personal stories and experiences. In Lichterman's own words, "Personalism does not necessarily deny the existence of communities surrounding and shaping the self, but it accentuates an individualized relationship to any such communities" (Lichterman 1996, p. 6).

3. The data set used for comparison is the National Household Education Surveys (NHES) Civic Involvement Surveys 1999. The NHES is a set of studies by the U.S. Department of Education's National Center for Education Statistics that surveys a nationally representative sample of 8,043 adolescents and young adults. In order to compare the NHES sample with the canvassers in this study—all of whom were at least 18 years old in the summer of 2003—only the data from the 384 participants in the youth component of the NHES who were 18 or older were included.

4. www.americorps.org/whoweare.html (accessed June 15, 2005).

5. The fellowship program places recent college graduates in advocacy positions for nine months of the year. During the summer, fellows are expected to direct canvass offices around the country.

6. See Skocpol (2004, p. 4). See also Skocpol (1996); Skocpol and Fiorina (1999); and Skocpol, Ganz, and Munson (2000).

7. Since my interview with him in 2003, drilling in the Arctic National Wildlife Refuge has been the subject of multiple political debates between Republicans and Democrats in Congress. In February 2006, President Bush included drilling in the refuge as part of his 2007 budget. It is unclear if the provision will make it through the budget approval process. See http://www.anwr.org/(accessed March 7, 2006). For earlier debates, see www.anwr.com/archives/revolt_of_gop_moderates_in_house_kills_anwr_for_now.php (accessed November 21, 2005).

8. These percentages are based on the survey component of the follow-up interview. For a detailed comparison of the canvassers' levels of civic engagement in 2004 with a national sample, see the Appendix.

9. This number (three months) does not include those who were working as canvass directors in the summer of 2003. The number is based on data collected during the follow-up interviews with two-thirds of the original cohort of summer 2003 canvassers. It is probable that those people who were still working for the organization in 2004 were more likely to participate in the follow-up interviews. The three-month figure likely overestimates the amount of time that the cohort worked for the organization.

10. This decision was based on my Memorandum of Understanding with the People's Project.

11. As it was, many of the participants in the follow-up component of this study did not initially remember participating in the study while they were working for the canvass in the summer of 2003.

12. This percentage was also reported by others, including a director in a different office who had been working for the organization for over two years and was still working with the organization in the summer of 2004.

13. Although I saw a diverse array of people arriving to interview for jobs, my agreement with the People's Project prevented me from speaking with them.

14. Those who had been working when the procedure was first instituted had to sign the agreement in order to receive their final paycheck. As of summer 2005, it was unclear whether the People's Project continued to have this requirement.

Notes to Chapter 4

1. For a discussion of the ways that funding for progressive causes is related to who is in the White House, see Dunlap and Catton (1994).

2. This number is calculated based on the members of America Votes, "a coalition of many of the largest membership-based groups in the country" who outsource their canvassing. See www.americavotes.org for more information (accessed September 27, 2005).

3. In some local chapter offices, there are no paid staff and the office is run entirely by volunteers.

4. This statistic is based on personal communication with Sally Green Heaven of the HRC. She reported that the other half of the groups' members came in from direct mail and telemarketing (May 26, 2005).

5. Putnam (1996, p. 2 of online version), www.prospect.org/print-friendly/print/V7/24/putnam-r.html (accessed March 7, 2006). See also Putnam (1995, 2000); Skocpol, Ganz, and Munson (2000).

6. www.savethechildren.org/mission/index.asp?stationpub=i_hpd-da2_au2&ArticleID=&NewsID= (accessed July 15, 2005).

7. For a history of the emergence of membership-based interest groups, see Clemens (1997).

8. Weir and Ganz (1997, p. 167).

9. See, for example, Berry (1999); Putnam (2000); Skocpol (1999, 2004).

10. Those members who volunteered in their local chapters, however, were involved locally.

11. Greenpeace is committed to relatively radical tactics to achieve its goals, including nonviolent civil disobedience and direct action.

12. Greenpeace has since experimented with other models of running its own indigenous canvass.

13. The exact number of campaigns and groups represented by the People's Project differs in each local office.

14. When I visited these offices in 2003, Baltimore had only four canvassers on staff and Ann Arbor had about fifteen.

15. In fact, it sometimes takes a family connection even to get an unpaid internship with a national group; and, while some of these internships offer a small stipend, most are unpaid.

16. The Sierra Club's national headquarters is located in San Francisco, California.

17. Some campus organizers are able to avoid directing a canvass by running campus-based programs over the summer.

18. www.greencorps.org (accessed July 19, 2005).

19. Personal communication with the author (May 26, 2005).

20. Miller (2004, p. 7).

21. See www.nonprofitwatch.org/greencorps (accessed September 15, 2005).

22. Personal communication with author, July 20, 2005. For more information, see www.nonprofitwatch.org/ (accessed November 22, 2005).

23. Miller (2004, p. 7).

24. www.greencorps.org/greencorps.asp?id2=4792&id3=greencorps& (accessed September 15, 2005).

25. Personal correspondence between former members of Green Corps and the author.

26. Skocpol, Ganz, and Munson (2000, p. 541). See also Skocpol (2003).

27. These canvassers referred to the noncompetition agreement that they signed. Because I was unable to see a copy of the agreement, it is unclear whether it did, in fact, limit the canvassers from working for these national groups after leaving the canvassing organization.

28. http://www.grassrootscampaigns.com/about.html (accessed May 13, 2004).

Notes to Chapter 5

1. Matt Bai, "The Multilevel Marketing of the President," *New York Times Magazine*, April 25, 2004, p. 44.

2. Ibid., p. 43.

3. For a summary of the Bipartisan Campaign Reform Act of 2002 in historical context, see the Campaign Legal Center's *Campaign Finance Guide*, http://www.campaignfinanceguide.org/ (accessed August 22, 2005).

4. Final resolution of these legal challenges came with the Supreme Court's decision to uphold the law in December 2003.

5. For a history of 527 groups, see the overview provided by the Brookings Institution at www.brookings.org/gs/cf/headlines/527_intro.htm (accessed August 22, 2005). For a list of 527 group activities during the 2004 election, see the Center for Public Integrity's online database, which lists the sources of the funds raised and how they were spent: www.publicintegrity. org/527/db.aspx?act=activity2003&sort=1 (accessed September 15, 2005).

6. Data on 527 fundraising and spending were provided by the Center for Public Integrity: www.publicintegrity.org/527/ (accessed August 26, 2005).

7. The official name of this group is the "Swift Vets and P.O.W.'s for Truth." See www.swiftvets.com/index.php (accessed August 22, 2005).

The amount spent is based on numbers provided on www.publicintegrity. org/527/db.aspx?act=activity2003&sort=1 (accessed September 15, 2005).

8. See Knott, Pilhofer, and Willis (2004), available at www.publicintegrity.org/527/report.aspx?aid=421&sid=200 (accessed August 22, 2005).

9. Matt Bai, "Machine Dreams: America Coming Together Is History," *New York Times Magazine*, August 21, 2005, pp. 11–12.

10. acthere.com/plan (accessed August 22, 2005).

11. Bill Bradley, "A Party Inverted," *New York Times*, March 30, 2005.

12. For a full discussion, see Balz and Brownstein (1996).

13. Ralph Reed, quoted in "Fighting for God and the Right Wing," *Time*, September 13, 1993, p. 58.

14. Reed is running for lieutenant governor of Georgia in 2006. There is some speculation that the 2006 election will begin his ascendance to the Georgia governorship and lead to a bid for the White House.

15. Jim Galloway, "GOP Whiz Enlisted to Grow Voter Database," *Atlanta Journal-Constitution*, December 21, 2003, p. A4; see also Joyce Purnick, "One-Doorbell-One-Vote Tactic Re-emerges in Bush-Kerry Race," *New York Times*, April 6, 2004, p. A1.

16. Indiana Republican Party, "72-Hour Plan," www.indgop.org/ commissioner/72hour.php (accessed August 25, 2005).

17. On college evangelicals, see Laurie Goodstein and David D. Kirkpatrick, "On a Christian Mission to the Top," *New York Times*, May 22, 2005, p. A1. On Christian rock, see, for example, John Leland, "At Festivals, Rock and T-Shirts Take Center Stage," *New York Times*, July 5, 2004, p. A10.

18. E-mail correspondence with the author, September 21, 2005. It is worth noting that, because so many people voted for Bush overall, the percentage of the youth vote in the 2004 election did not change from 2000.

19. Bai, "The Multilevel Marketing of the President."

20. Purnick, "One-Doorbell-One-Vote Tactic."

21. Most electoral canvassers do not raise funds. Rather, they are paid to register potential Democratic voters and mobilize them to vote.

22. Examples of such locally embedded civil society institutions are discussed in Sirianni and Friedland (2001). See also Boyte (2004).

23. Center for the Study of Elections and Democracy (2004, p. 2).

24. www.emilyslist.org/about/ (accessed August 29, 2005). Joe Solmonese left EMILY's List to become the president of the Human Rights Cam-

paign in March 2005.

25. For a similar account of the pro-life and pro-choice movements, see McCarthy (1987).

26. This program also organized volunteers from nontargeted areas to adopt areas in swing states.

27. See www.moveonpac.org/lnvb/ (accessed August 26, 2005).

28. The numbers presented here are based on the Center for the Study of Elections and Democracy Press Release, "527s Had a Substantial Impact on the Ground and Air Wars in 2004, December 16, 2004, available at csed.byu.edu/pressreleases.html (accessed March 7, 2006).

29. Bai, "Machine Dreams," p. 11.

30. For the full text, see www.blogforamerica.com/archives/003001.html (accessed August 25, 2005), and for a copy of the commercial, see the Club for Growth's website: www.clubforgrowth.org/pastproject.php (accessed August 25, 2005).

31. It is worth noting that shared norms are seen as a central component of a vibrant community that is rich in social capital. See especially Putnam (1995, 1996, 2000); see also Bellah et al. (1996).

32. See www.indgop.org/commissioner/72hour.php.

33. Bai, "The Multilevel Marketing of the President."

34. I was unable to gain access to this research.

35. Matt Bai, "Who Lost Ohio?" *New York Times Magazine*, November 21, 2004, p. 67.

Notes to Chapter 6

1. See Putnam (2000, p. 19).

2. See, e.g., Laurie Goodstein and David D. Kirkpatrick, "On a Christian Mission to the Top," *New York Times*, May 22, 2005, p. A1; Jeff Horwitz, "My Right-Wing Degree," Salon.com, May 25, 2005; Hanna Rosin, "God and Country: A College That Trains Young Christians to Be Politicians," *New Yorker*, June 27, 2005.

3. Some scholars have argued that democracy is not about passive consumption, but about public work. See especially Boyte (2004). See also Barber (1998); Mathews (1994).

4. This amount of time was calculated for the canvassers who were not directing the campaign offices.

5. Boyte (2004, p. 2).

6. For a discussion, see Skocpol (1999, pp. 461–510); Skocpol (2003); Skocpol (2004).

7. See, e.g., Bellah et al. (1996); Putnam (1995, 1996, 2000); Weir and Ganz (1997).

8. For an overview of these debates, see Coats and Santorum (1998); Ehrenhalt (1998); Skocpol (1998, 2003); Solo and Pressberg (1998).

9. Coats and Santorum (1998, p. 105).

10. Clemens (1997, p. 13).

11. See, for example, Denning (1997); McAdam (1988); Payne and NetLibrary Inc. (1995).

12. Although a small handful of candidates have connected to Democratic voters through their civic experiences (such as former president Bill Clinton and Senator Barack Obama of Illinois), they are increasingly rare.

13. Bradley (1998, p. 114).

14. See Boyte (2004); Sirianni and Friedland (2001); see also Solo and Pressberg (1998).

15. This list is not meant to be exhaustive, it is merely a sample of groups that would likely have members who support the progressive platform.

16. For example, Ladd (1999). See also DiIulio (1998); Rivers (1998); Schambra (1998); Wuthnow (1994). Religious assemblies that are likely to be more supportive of Democratic candidates include, but are not limited to, Buddhists, Reform Jews, Quakers, and Unitarians.

Notes to Appendix

1. Lofland and Lofland (1995, p. 5).

2. All stages of the data collection, including the initial interviews at the canvass offices in 2003 and the follow-up phone interviews in 2004, were conducted with the assistance of graduate research assistants.

3. Ten people from the original sample, or about 9 percent, were not willing to be contacted for a follow-up interview and did not provide contact information.

4. This percentage is based on the number of people who participated in the follow-up component of the study versus those who said they were willing to participate.

5. I also contacted clients listed on the website of the Project's spinoff organization, Grassroots Campaigns (accessed May 13, 2004).

6. See Oesterle, Johnson, and Mortimer (2004).

7. Since most had been working for the canvass for only a short time, it is probable that they came to the canvass with these preexisting characteristics (for all of the canvassers in the sample who were not directing offices, the median time working for the People's Project was only twenty days).

References

Almond, Gabriel Abraham, and Sidney Verba. 1963. *The Civic Culture: Political Attitudes and Democracy in Five Nations*. Princeton, N.J.: Princeton University Press.

Balz, Daniel J., and Ronald Brownstein. 1996. *Storming the Gates: Protest Politics and the Republican Revival*. Boston, Mass.: Little, Brown.

Barber, Benjamin R. 1998. *A Place for Us: How to Make Society Civil and Democracy Strong*. New York: Hill and Wang.

Bartell, T., and S. Bouxsein. 1973. "Chelsea Project-Candidate Preference, Issue Preference, and Turnout Effects of Student Canvassing." *Public Opinion Quarterly* 37: 268–75.

Bellah, Robert N., Richard Madsen, William M. Sullivan, Ann Swidler, and Steven M. Tipton. 1996. *Habits of the Heart: Individualism and Commitment in American Life*. Updated ed. Berkeley: University of California Press.

Berry, Jeffrey M. 1997. *The Interest Group Society*. New York: Longman.

———. 1999. "The Rise of Citizen Groups." In *Civic Engagement in American Democracy*, edited by T. Skocpol and M. P. Fiorina, pp. 367–93. Washington, D.C.: Brookings Institution Press and Russell Sage Foundation.

Bourdieu, Pierre. 1986. "The Forms of Capital." In *Handbook of Theory and Research for the Sociology of Education*, edited by J. G. Richardson, pp. 241–58. New York: Greenwood Press.

Boyte, Harry Chatten. 2004. *Everyday Politics: Reconnecting Citizens and Public Life*. Philadelphia: University of Pennsylvania Press.

Boyte, Harry Chatten and Nancy N. Kari. 1996. *Building America: The Democratic Promise of Public Work*. Philadelphia: Temple University Press.

Boyte, Harry Chatten, Heather Booth, and Steve Max. 1986. *Citizen Action and the New American Populism*. Philadelphia: Temple University Press.

Bradley, Bill. 1998. "America's Challenge: Revitalizing Our National Community." In *Community Works: The Revival of Civil Society in America*, edited by E. J. Dionne, pp. 107–14. Washington, D.C.: Brookings Institution Press.

Clemens, Elisabeth Stephanie. 1997. *The People's Lobby: Organizational Innovation and the Rise of Interest Group Politics in the United States, 1890–1925.* Chicago, Ill.: University of Chicago Press.

Coats, Dan, and Rick Santorum. 1998. "Civil Society and the Humble Role of Government." In *Community Works: The Revival of Civil Society in America*, edited by E. J. Dionne, pp. 101–06. Washington, D.C.: Brookings Institution Press.

Coleman, J. S. 1988. "Social Capital in the Creation of Human-Capital." *American Journal of Sociology* 94: S95–S120.

Denning, Michael. 1996. *The Cultural Front: The Laboring of American Culture in the Twentieth Century.* London: Verso.

DiIulio, John J., Jr. 1998. "The Lord's Work: The Church and Civil Society." In *Community Works: The Revival of Civil Society in America*, edited by E. J. Dionne, pp. 50–58. Washington, D.C.: Brookings Institution Press.

Dunlap, Riley E., and William R. Catton Jr. 1994. "Struggling with Human Exemptionalism: The Rise, Decline and Revitalization of Environmental Sociology." *American Sociologist* 5: 243–73.

Eckstein, S. 2001. "Community as Gift-Giving: Collectivistic Roots of Volunteerism." *American Sociological Review* 66: 829–51.

Edelman, Murray J. 1964. *The Symbolic Uses of Politics.* Urbana: University of Illinois Press.

Edwards, B., and M. W. Foley. 1998. "Civil Society and Social Capital beyond Putnam." *American Behavioral Scientist* 42: 124–39.

Ehrenhalt, Alan. 1998. "Where Have All the Followers Gone?" In *Community Works: The Revival of Civil Society in America*, edited by E. J. Dionne, pp. 93–98. Washington, D.C.: Brookings Institution Press.

Eliasoph, Nina. 1998. *Avoiding Politics: How Americans Produce Apathy in Everyday Life.* Cambridge: Cambridge University Press.

Fiorina, Morris P. 1999. "Extreme Voices: A Dark Side of Civic Engagement." In *Civic Engagement in American Democracy*, edited by T. Skocpol and M. P. Fiorina, pp. 395–426. Washington, D.C.: Brookings Institution Press.

Frank, Thomas. 2004. *What's the Matter with Kansas? How Conservatives Won the Heart of America.* New York: Metropolitan Books.

Green, Donald P., and Alan S. Gerber. 2004. *Get Out the Vote!* Washington, D.C.: Brookings Institution Press.

Green, Donald P., Alan S. Gerber, and David W. Nickerson. 2003. "Getting Out the Vote in Local Elections: Results from Six Door-to-Door Canvassing Experiments." *Journal of Politics* 65, no. 4: 1083–96.

Green, John C. 2004. "The American Religious Landscape and Politics, 2004." Report from the Pew Forum on Religion & Public Life, Washington, D.C. September 9. Available at pewforum.org/docs/index.php?DocID=55 (accessed March 7, 2006).

Huckfeldt, Robert, and John Sprague. 1992. "Political Parties and Electoral Mobilization: Political Structure, Social Structure and the Party Canvass." *American Political Science Review* 86, no. 1: 70–86.

Indiana Republican Party. 2005. "72-Hour Plan." Indiana Republican Party, Indianapolis.

Keeter, Scott, Cliff Zukin, Molly Andolina, and Krista Jenkins. 2002. "The Civic and Political Health of the Nation: A Generational Portrait." Pew Research Center for the People and the Press, George Mason University, Fairfax, Virginia.

Knott, Alex, Aron Pilhofer, and Derek Willis. 2004. "GOP 527s Outspend Dems in Late Ad Blitz: Progress for America and Swift Boats Dominated Airwaves in Swing States." Washington, D.C.: Center for Public Integrity. Available at www.publicintegrity.org/527/report.aspx?aid=421&sid=200 (accessed March 7, 2006).

Ladd, Everett Carll. 1999. *The Ladd Report.* New York: Free Press.

Lakoff, George. 2004. *Don't Think of an Elephant! Know Your Values and Frame the Debate: The Essential Guide for Progressives.* White River Junction, Vt.: Chelsea Green.

Levine, Peter, and Mark Hugo Lopez. 2002. "Youth Voter Turnout Has Declined, by Any Measure." Report from the Center for Information and Research on Civic Learning and Engagement (CIRCLE): College Park, Md.

Lichterman, Paul. 1996. *The Search for Political Community: American Activists Reinventing Commitment.* Cambridge: Cambridge University Press.

Lofland, John, and Lyn H. Lofland. 1995. *Analyzing Social Settings: A Guide to Qualitative Observation and Analysis.* Belmont, Calif.: Wadsworth.

Martin, Rod. 2002. "Quiet Revolution: The Christianization of the Republican Party." *Christian Statesman* 145, no. 6. Available at www.natreformassn.org/statesman/02/TOC145-6.html (accessed March 7, 2006)

Mathews, Forrest David. 1994. *Politics for People: Finding a Responsible Public Voice.* Urbana: University of Illinois Press.

McAdam, Doug. 1988. *Freedom Summer.* New York: Oxford University Press.

McCarthy, John D. 1987. "Pro-Life and Pro-Choice Mobilization: Infrastructure Deficits and New Technologies." In *Social Movements in an Organizational Society,* edited by Mayer N. Zald and John D. McCarthy, pp. 49–67. New Brunswick, N.J.: Transaction.

McDonald, M. P., and S. L. Popkin. 2001. "The Myth of the Vanishing Voter." *American Political Science Review* 95: 963–74.

Miller, Nathaniel. 2004. "The Problem with Green Corps." *Threshold* (Winter): 7–9.

Minkoff, Debra C. 1997. "Producing Social Capital: National Social Movements and Civil Society." *American Behavioral Scientist* (Mar./Apr.): 606–30.

Morlan, Robert Loren. 1955. *Political Prairie Fire: The Nonpartisan League, 1915–1922.* Minneapolis: University of Minnesota Press.

Nie, Norman H., Sidney Verba, and John R. Petrocik. 1979. *The Changing American Voter.* Cambridge, Mass.: Harvard University Press.

Oesterle, S., M. K. Johnson, and J. T. Mortimer. 2004. "Volunteerism during the Transition to Adulthood: A Life Course Perspective." *Social Forces* 82: 1123–49.

Ortega, Bob. 1998. *In Sam We Trust: The Untold Story of Sam Walton and How Wal-Mart Is Devouring America.* New York: Times Business.

Paxton, Pamela. 1999. "Is Social Capital Declining in the United States? A Multiple Indicator Assessment." *American Journal of Sociology* 105: 88–127.

———. 2002. "Social Capital and Democracy: An Interdependent Relationship." *American Sociological Review* 67: 254–77.

Payne, Charles M., and NetLibrary Inc. 1995. *I've Got the Light of Freedom: The Organizing Tradition and the Mississippi Freedom Struggle.* Berkeley: University of California Press.

Piven, Frances Fox, and Richard A. Cloward. 1988. *Why Americans Don't Vote.* New York: Pantheon Books.

———. 2000. *Why Americans Still Don't Vote: And Why Politicians Want It That Way.* Boston, Mass.: Beacon Press.

Portes, Alejandro. 1998. "Social Capital: Its Orgins and Applications in Modern Sociology." *Annual Review of Sociology* 24: 1–24.

Putnam, Robert D. 1995. "Bowling Alone: America's Declining Social Capital." *Journal of Democracy* 6: 65–78.

―――. 1996. "The Strange Disappearance of Civic America." *American Prospect* 7 (December). Available at www.prospect.org/print-friendly/print/ V7/24/putnam-r.html.

―――. 2000. *Bowling Alone*. New York: Simon and Schuster.

Reiter, H. L. 1979. "Why Is Turnout Down?" *Public Opinion Quarterly* 43: 297–311.

Rivers, Eugene F. III. 1998. "High-Octane Faith and Civil Society." In *Community Works: The Revival of Civil Society in America*, edited by E. J. Dionne, pp. 59–63. Washington, D.C.: Brookings Institution Press.

Rotolo, T. 1999. "Trends in Voluntary Association Participation." *Nonprofit and Voluntary Sector Quarterly* 28: 199–212.

Schambra, William A. 1998. "All Community Is Local: The Key to America's Civic Renewal." In *Community Works: The Revival of Civil Society in America*, edited by E. J. Dionne, pp. 59–63. Washington, D.C.: Brookings Institution Press.

Schlozman, Kay Lehman, and John T. Tierney. 1986. *Organized Interests and American Democracy*. New York: Harper and Row.

Schofer, E., and M. Fourcade-Gourinchas. 2001. "The Structural Contexts of Civic Engagement: Voluntary Association Membership in Comparative Perspective." *American Sociological Review* 66: 806–28.

Sirianni, Carmen, and Lewis Friedland. 2001. *Civic Innovation in America*. Berkeley: University of California Press.

Skocpol, Theda. 1996. "Unravelling from Above." *American Prospect* (March–April): 20–25.

―――. 1998. "Don't Blame Big Government: America's Voluntary Groups." In *Community Works: The Revival of Civil Society in America*, edited by E. J. Dionne, pp. 37–43. Washington, D.C.: Brookings Institution Press.

―――. 1999. "Advocates without Members: The Recent Transformation of American Civic Life." In *Civic Engagement in American Democracy*, edited by T. Skocpol and M. P. Fiorina, pp. 37–43. Washington, D.C.: Brookings Institution Press.

―――. 2003. *Diminished Democracy: From Membership to Management in American Civic Life*. Norman: University of Oklahoma Press.

―――. 2004. "Voice and Inequality: The Transformation of American Civic Democracy." *Perspectives on Politics* 2, no. 1: 3–20.

Skocpol, Theda, and Morris P. Fiorina, eds. 1999. *Civic Engagement in American Democracy*. Washington, D.C.: Brookings Institution Press.

Skocpol, Theda, Marshall Ganz, and Ziad Munson. 2000. "A Nation of Organizers: The Institutional Origins of Civic Voluntarism in the United States." *American Political Science Review* 94: 527–46.

Solo, Pam, and Gail Pressberg. 1998. "Beyond Theory: Civil Society in Action." In *Community Works: The Revival of Civil Society in America*, edited by E. J. Dionne, pp. 81–87. Washington, D.C.: Brookings Institution Press.

Tocqueville, Alexis de. [1876] 1966. *Democracy in America*. New Rochelle, N.Y.: Arlington House.

Verba, Sidney, Kay Lehman Schlozman, and Henry E. Brady. 1995. *Voice and Equality: Civic Voluntarism in American Politics*. Cambridge, Mass.: Harvard University Press.

Walker, Jack L. 1991. *Mobilizing Interest Groups in America: Patrons, Professions, and Social Movements*. Ann Arbor: University of Michigan Press.

Weir, Margaret, and Marshall Ganz. 1997. "Reconnecting People and Politics." In *The New Majority: Toward a Popular Progressive Politics*, edited by S. B. Greenberg and T. Skocpol, pp. 149–71. New Haven, Conn.: Yale University Press.

Wuthnow, Robert. 1991. *Between States and Markets: The Voluntary Sector in Comparative Perspective*. Princeton, N.J.: Princeton University Press.

———. 1994. *Sharing the Journey: Support Groups and America's New Quest for Community*. New York: Free Press.

———. 1998. *Loose Connections: Joining Together in America's Fragmented Communities*. Cambridge, Mass.: Harvard University Press.

Wuthnow, Robert, and NetLibrary Inc. 1998. *After Heaven: Spirituality in America since the 1950s*. Berkeley: University of California Press.

Index